THE NEXT GREAT WAVE

OBJECT-RELATIONAL DBMS

THE NEXT GREAT WAVE

OBJECT-RELATIONAL DBMS

MICHAEL STONEBRAKER

WITH DOROTHY MOORE

MORGAN KAUFMANN PUBLISHERS, INC., SAN FRANCISCO, CALIFORNIA

Sponsoring Editors Bruce M. Spatz/Michael B. Morgan
Production Manager Yonie Overton
Production Editor Julie Pabst
Editorial Assistant Jane Elliott
Cover Design Carron Design
Cover Photograph Alex Williams/Masterfile
Proofreader Ken DellaPenta
Printer Port City Press

This book was typeset in FrameMaker by Dorothy Moore.

Morgan Kaufmann Publishers, Inc.
Editorial and Sales Office
340 Pine Street, Sixth Floor
San Francisco, CA 94104-3205
USA
Telephone 415/392-2665
Facsimile 415/982-2665
Internet mkp@mkp.com
Order toll free 800/745-7323

Library of Congress Cataloging-in-Publication Data is available for this book.

ISBN 1-55860-397-2

Contents

Preface

This book explores a new and promising class of database management systems, the object-relational DBMS. The spectrum of application areas covered by the object-relational DBMS ranges from video and graphic asset management in the entertainment industry to time series analysis problems in the financial services market, scientific databases, and geographic information systems (GISs). In addition, the exploding market for multimedia data, often accessed through the World Wide Web, is best served by object-relational technology. This book explains why object-relational DBMSs will replace relational systems to become the next great wave of database technology.

This book was written primarily for application programmers and information services (IS) managers who want to understand how this new technology fits into their environments. It contains many examples and tables to help you make informed decisions about object-relational systems.

Chapter 1 begins by introducing a two-by-two matrix for classifying all DBMS applications. File systems, relational DBMSs, object-oriented DBMSs, and object-relational DBMSs are each represented by a quadrant of the matrix. Not only is the matrix a handy way to classify DBMS applications, but it also provides a perspective on where object-relational DBMSs fit in the database world.

Chapters 2–7 explain the following four main features of an object-relational DBMS:

- support for base type extension in an SQL context
- support for complex objects in an SQL context
- support for inheritance in an SQL context
- support for a production rule system

The book also describes the specific requirements needed to fully support each of these features.

Chapter 2 discusses base type extension, and Chapter 3 provides several specific examples of the concept. Chapter 4 provides the support requirements for complex objects in an object-relational DBMS. The following type constructors are needed to build complex types:

- record of objects
- sets of objects
- references (pointers) to objects

However, there are other plausible type constructors, and some of the more important ones are described in Chapter 5. Chapter 6 continues with a discussion of inheritance and indicates the requirements for an object-relational DBMS to fully support this concept. The last required feature, a rules system, is the subject of Chapter 7.

While the first half of the book discusses the required features of an object-relational DBMS, the second half of the book focuses on the actual mechanisms required to support an object-relational DBMS engine. Chapter 8 covers parser requirements, and Chapters 9 and 10 discuss optimizer requirements. Chapter 9 describes how a traditional relational optimizer operates; Chapter 10 indicates the changes that must be made to turn a traditional optimizer into a good object-relational one. Because most vendors are not forthcoming about the quality of their optimizers, the chapter also includes a collection of tests you can perform to discover the relative merit of the optimizer in any target system. Chapter 11 finishes the implementation discussion with a treatment of rule systems.

As you will discover in Chapters 8–11, a relational engine must be largely rewritten to include object-relational functionality. Chapter 12 lists the available technical options for comercial vendors and indicates which option certain vendors have taken.

Chapters 13 and 14 look at a vexing problem that many users of DBMS technology will face in the future—what do you do if you have a "multi-quadrant" application, one that exhibits the characteristics of more than one box in Chapter 1's matrix?

Two examples of such multi-quadrant problems are given in Chapter 13. Chapter 14 offers available solution possibilities.

No book on DBMS technology is complete without a discussion of database design. Chapter 15 shows that the challenges of designing for a standard relational database are increased with the more general data model presented by the object-relational DBMS. To conclude, Chapter 16 surveys the current marketplace and looks at how successfully, or unsuccessfully, current products match up to a list of required features for an object-relational DBMS. Because rapid progress is being made in this field, you are advised to check with specific vendors for updated descriptions of products of interest.

This book pays little attention to traditional DBMS services, such as concurrency control, crash recovery, views, protection, replication, parallelism, and distributed DBMS support. These topics are crucially important for any DBMS, regardless of its data model and query language. In fact, many lump this collection of features into a single requirement—that the DBMS must scale to large numbers of users and large amounts of data. Because object-relational DBMSs introduce no new spin on these services, they are not explored in this book in the interest of brevity. Instead, the book focuses exclusively on defining the functionality of an object-relational DBMS.

Throughout the book, there are examples of object-relational features, typically expressed in SQL. The question naturally arises, ''Which SQL should I use?'' There are draft SQL documents on both SQL-3 from the ANSI X3H2 SQL committee (Melton 1995) and OQL from the Object Database Management Group (ODMG) (Cattell 1995). Unfortunately, these standards are evolving rapidly and, as a result, the details change many times a year. Alternatively, there are extended SQL systems from a variety of commercial vendors. This book uses the SQL currently implemented by the Illustra DBMS because it will seemingly have a longer lifetime than the current draft standards.

Two liberties are taken in this book with respect to Illustra SQL. First, for readability, the book relaxes the restriction that operators cannot have alphabetical characters. Second, for ease of explanation, the book uses the syntax for sets in Illustra's upcoming Version 3, instead of the current Version 2.

To further explore many of the concepts in this book, please contact Illustra Information Technologies, Inc., 1111 Broadway, Suite 2000, Oakland, CA 94607. Telephone Illustra at (510) 652-8000, or send email to info@illustra.com. Visit Illustra's home page at http://www.illustra.com.

CHAPTER 1

The DBMS Matrix

This chapter presents an overview of database management systems (DBMSs) from both technical and marketplace perspectives. To help in classifying applications that require DBMSs, this chapter introduces a matrix; each quadrant in the matrix represents one of four general types of DBMSs. This chapter also examines the types of problems each kind of DBMS solves and where various DBMS products fit in today's marketplace. One size does not fit all in the database world. In other words, there is no single DBMS that solves the requirements of all applications.

1.1   *A DBMS Classification Matrix*

The two-by-two matrix for classifying DBMSs is illustrated in Figure 1.1. In the matrix, the horizontal axis shows simple data on the left and complex data on the right. Of course, in the real world, the complexity of an application's data can vary. However, for the sake of example, assume there are only two possibilities, simple and complex. The vertical axis differentiates whether the application requires a query capability. Again, for simplicity, assume there are only two choices, "query" and "no query."

Depending on its characteristics, an application fits into at least one of the four quadrants in Figure 1.1. Of course, many applications have qualities that place them in more than one quadrant. Multi-quadrant applications are explored in Chapter 13. For now, assume that an application can be placed into a single quadrant.

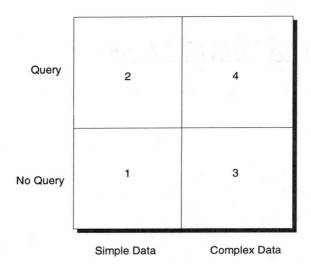

FIGURE 1.1   A Matrix for Classifying DBMS Applications

Quadrant 1, which holds applications having simple data without queries, is examined first.

1.2   *Quadrant 1: Simple Data without Queries*

Consider a standard text processing system such as *Word*, *Framemaker*, *Word Perfect*, *vi*, or *emacs*. All enable you to open a file by name, which results in the contents of the file being copied into virtual memory. You can then edit the file and update the virtual memory object. At intervals, the object is saved to disk storage. When you are finished, you can close the file, causing the virtual memory copy to be stored back to the file system.

A text editor qualifies as a "no query" application that does not need or use SQL. (The only "query" made by a text editor is "get file," and the only "update" is "put file.") In addition, a text editor is appropriately served by the data model available in the file system, namely a sequence of characters of arbitrary length. A text editor is a "no query-simple data" application that fits into quadrant 1, the lower-left quadrant of the two-by-two matrix. (In the future, it is quite possible that text editors will move to one of the other matrix quadrants, because over time the data model of text editors is getting more complex as documents become structured with embedded reports, graphs, and spreadsheets.)

A quick point before proceeding: text editors are being discussed here, not more sophisticated groupware products, such as *Lotus Notes*. Document management systems, such as *Documentum*, are also not included in the discussion. Such products have to be independently placed in an appropriate quadrant in the matrix.

The obvious DBMS for applications in the lower-left quadrant of the matrix is the file system provided by the operating system vendor for the hardware in question. In fact, virtually all text editors use this primitive level of DBMS service, and their developers have no plans to move to anything more sophisticated. If you have no need for queries and no need for complex data, then the service provided by the file system is perfectly adequate. Moreover, a file system invariably has higher performance than any more sophisticated system. The bottom line is simple: if you don't need the service, then there is no need to pay for it in terms of lower performance.

1.3   *Quadrant 2: Simple Data with Queries*

A well-known database example nicely illustrates the upper-left corner of the matrix. Suppose you want to store the following information about each employee in a hypothetical company: the employee's name, start date, salary, and department. In addition, you require the name, floor number, and budget for each of the departments in the company. You can capture the schema for all of this information with the following standard SQL statements:

```
create table emp (
                name        varchar (30),
                startdate   date,
                salary      float,
                dept        varchar (20));

create table dept (
                dname       varchar (20),
                budget      float,
                floor       int);
```

Notice that the above tables contain a collection of structured records, each with attributes that are simple integers, floats, dates, and character strings—all standard data types found in SQL-92. This data can therefore be classified as "simple."

After you create the schema, you can form the following questions quite naturally in SQL:

1. Find the names of employees with an employment start date after 1980 and who earn more than $40,000.

```
select name
from emp
where startdate > '1980-12-31' and salary > 40000;
```

2. Find the names of employees who work on the first floor.

```
select name
from emp
where dept in
            (select dname
            from dept
            where floor = 1);
```

3. Find the average salary of employees in the marketing department.

```
select avg(salary)
from emp
where dept = 'marketing';
```

Applications with simple data and queries that are easily expressed in standard SQL-92 tend to be identified as "business data processing" applications, and they are a natural fit for the upper-left quadrant of the matrix. Such applications have the following requirements:

Query Language. SQL-89 is a requirement. It is desirable to also have the newer SQL-92 standard.

Client Tools. A tool kit that enables a programmer to set up *forms* for data entry and display is required. This tool kit must also enable sequencing between forms through control flow logic. Such tool kits are called fourth-generation languages (4GLs). Example 4GLs include *PowerBuilder* from Sybase, *Visual Basic* from Microsoft, *Windows/4GL* from Computer Associates, *SQL-Forms* from Oracle, and products from Easel, Gupta, and Progress. In fact, there are at least 75 4GLs on the market today, all offering similar capabilities. Moreover, it is not a significant stretch to call *Lotus Notes* a 4GL.

In addition, client tools must include a report writer, a database design tool, a performance monitor, and the ability to call DBMS services from a variety of third-generation languages (for example, C, FORTRAN, or COBOL).

Performance. Much of the business data processing marketplace entails transaction processing where many simultaneous users submit requests for DBMS services from client terminals or PCs. User interactions tend to be fairly simple SQL statements with many updates. When parallel conflicting updates are processed by a DBMS, then the user requires a predictable outcome. This has led to the notion of two-phase locking, which ensures so-called serializability. (If you are unfamiliar with the concept of two-phase locking, consult a standard textbook on DBMSs, such as Date [1985], Korth and Silberschatz [1986] or Ullman [1980].) In addition, there is an absolute requirement to never lose the user's data, regardless of what kind of failure might have occurred. These include disk crashes as well as operating system failures. Providing recovery from crashes is typically provided through write-ahead log (WAL) technology. (If you are interested in this topic, consult any of the standard textbooks mentioned above.) Together, two-phase locking and a write-ahead log provide transaction management; that is, user queries and updates are grouped into units of work called transactions. Each transaction is atomic (it either happens completely or not at all), serializable (appears to have happened before or after all other parallel transactions), and durable (once committed, its effect can never be lost). Transaction management is a sophisticated subject; a definitive reference on the subject is *Transaction Processing: Concepts and Techniques* (Gray and Reuter 1993).

Security/Architecture. Because users put sensitive data, such as salaries, into business data processing databases, DBMSs must be secure. The DBMS must run in a separate address space from the client application with a user ID that is separate from any application. Actual data files utilized in the database are specified as readable and writable only by the DBMS. This client-server architecture, shown in Figure 1.2, is a requirement of upper-left quadrant applications.

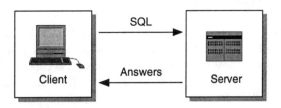

FIGURE 1.2   Standard Client-Server Architecture

In any case, for upper-left quadrant applications, the user requires an SQL DBMS optimized for transaction processing that supports many simultaneous users with simple commands. A standard benchmark that typifies this sort of interaction is TPC-C from the Transaction Processing Council. TPC-C is discussed at length in *The Benchmark Handbook for Database and Transaction Processing Systems* (Gray 1993). There is a movement over time toward more complex transactions, and TPC has responded with a more stringent standard, TPC-D.

The SQL DBMS Market: A Crowded Playing Field

The general checklist of requirements for an SQL DBMS with 4GL client tools optimized for transaction processing is met very well by the many relational DBMS vendors. The main ones are Oracle, Sybase, Informix, and CA-Ingres. In addition, hardware vendors such as Tandem, Hewlett-Packard, and IBM offer relational database products.

These products differ mainly on detailed features; from a distance they all look very similar. To distinguish their products, all vendors engage in considerable marketing hype touting their respective wares. Business data processing is a large and competitive market and vendors have their hands full with the following Herculean demands for the perfect DBMS:

- It must run well on shared memory multiprocessors.
- It must interface to every transaction monitor.
- It must run on every hardware platform.
- It must provide a gateway to all the other vendors' DBMSs.
- It must provide parallel execution of user queries.
- It must solve the "32-bit barrier," that is, run well on very large databases.
- It must provide "7 times 24" service, that is, never require taking the database off-line for maintenance.

Despite the crowded playing field, the relational DBMS vendors are generally very healthy companies. Relational DBMS customers have a seemingly insatiable need for additional licenses, add-on products, and consulting services. Collectively, the relational DBMS market is approximately $8 billion per year and growing at more than 25% per year.

The only storm cloud on the horizon is the imminent arrival of Microsoft into this market. They have acquired the Sybase code line for Microsoft Windows NT and have a substantial group in Redmond improving it. Many would argue that Microsoft SQL server is now a superior product on Microsoft Windows NT. Besides having a good product, Microsoft is committed to "PC pricing" for database systems. They are undercutting the pricing structure of the traditional vendors and generally causing relational DBMS license prices to fall. Look for continued erosion of pricing in this market.

1.4   *Quadrant 3: Complex Data without Queries*

The next application fits in the lower-right quadrant of the matrix. In this example, suppose the user is the facilities planner for a company that has an "open floor plan." Nobody gets an office; instead, all the company's employees are arranged into cubicles with partitions separating them. Hewlett-Packard uses this open floor plan. In such a company, departments grow and shrink as employees get hired, are transferred, or quit. Over time, the arrangement of employees on the physical real estate of the building becomes suboptimal, and a global rearrangement of space is warranted. This "garbage collection" of free space and concurrent rearrangement of employees is the target application in this example.

The database for the application can be expressed in the following SQL commands:

```
create table employee (
                    name            varchar (30),
                    space           polygon,
                    adjacency       set-of (employee));

create table floors (
                    number          int,
                    asf             swiss-cheese-polygon);
```

For each employee, the employee's name, current cubicle location (space), and the set of all other employees who share a common cubicle wall with the employee (adjacency) will be recorded.

For each floor, the floor number and the amount of assignable square feet (asf) will be recorded. The asf is the building's outline minus the rest rooms, elevator shafts, and fire exits. It is a polygon with "holes" in it, a "swiss cheese polygon."

Clearly, this data is much more complex than the emp and dept data discussed on page 3. Because of its complex data, place the floor plan application on the right side of Figure 1.1 on page 2.

The application can be pseudo-coded as follows:

```
main ()
{
read all employees;
read all floors;
compact();
write all employees;
}
```

Here, the program must read all employee records to ascertain current spaces for
employees and it must get the asf for each floor. The program will build some sort
of virtual memory structure for the next step of the program. The program's compaction routine then walks the virtual memory structure, perhaps many times, to
generate a revised allocation of employees into the asf on each floor. When compaction is complete, each employee record must be rewritten with a new space allocation.

Obviously, this program reads the entirety of both data collections, computes on
this collection, and then writes one collection. It is analogous to the text editor that
read, computed, and then wrote a single file (page 2). As with the text editor example, there is not a query in sight in this program. Unlike the text editor example, the
data involved in this application is rather complex. Thus, this program qualifies as a
lower-right quadrant application—one without queries but with complex data.

While the garbage collection/compaction example may seem somewhat artificial, it
is, in fact, very representative of most electronic CAD (computer-aided design)
applications. In a typical ECAD application, a chip design is stored on disk as a
complex object, read into main memory, compacted by an optimization program,
and then written back to persistent storage. Applications that find power consump-
tion or timing faults have a similar structure. The office floor plan application, however, is a simple application that is more easily understood than the details of an
ECAD program.

Using a traditional file system for the floor plan application is tedious. The application must manually read the employee and floor information. Converting the data
from disk format to main memory format is even more taxing. The adjacency information is a set of employees that can be represented on disk as a set of unique identifiers for employees. These unique identifiers are converted to virtual memory
pointers during the load process. Because virtual memory pointers are transient and
depend on where the data is actually loaded in memory, they cannot be reused in
subsequent executions of the program. Disk pointers are fundamentally different
from main memory pointers, and the load process must convert from one to the
other. Similarly, when the data is written back to disk, the adjacency information

may have been changed by the compaction routine, requiring a reverse conversion from main memory to disk representation.

Loading and converting the data, and then unloading and reconverting it, is a time-consuming effort that must be done by the person developing the compaction routine if the developer is using a file system as a storage engine for the application. A much better solution is to support persistent storage for the programming language in which *compact* is written.

Assuming that this language is C++, *compact* would have a collection of data structures defined for its computation. One such declaration is

```
integer I;
```

In a normal programming language I is a transient variable. In other words, it has no value until it is initialized by the program and its value is lost when the program terminates. Suppose persistent variables are utilized in *compact*, declared as follows:

```
persistent integer J;
```

Because J is persistent, its value is automatically saved when the compaction program terminates. This value is also automatically available when the program is restarted the next time. With persistent variables, it becomes the language support system's problem to load and unload data as well as to convert it from disk format to main memory format and back. The person writing the compaction routine need only write the algorithm and is freed from other details.

A persistent programming language offers the best DBMS support for this compaction application. With such a language, you can move away from writing the following code:

```
main ()
{
read all employees;
read all floors;
compact();
write all employees;
}
```

to merely having to code

```
main ()
{
compact();
}
```

A persistent programming language is fundamentally very closely integrated with a specific language. Clearly, the persistence system must understand the specific data declarations of the target language. Thus, if someone is developing the *compact* routine in COBOL, then persistent COBOL is required and persistent C++ is completely useless. In short, one persistence system is required for each language.

Notice that our application has the following DBMS requirements:

Query Language. None is required for this application. If one exists, it serves no useful purpose.

Client Tools. The writer of *compact* is presumably using some sort of programming language tool kit such as the one from ParcPlace or NeXt. Client tools need not be a major focus for a persistent storage company because typically the writer expects to obtain client tools from a programming language productivity company.

Performance. The fundamental performance problem that this application needs to solve is to keep up with a non-persistent version. For example, if a user runs *compact* on "vanilla" C++ and handles storage management, then the user obtains a certain performance. If the user moves *compact* on top of a persistent language, then the user wishes *compact* to run no more than (say) 10% slower than the non-persistent case.

Security/Architecture. Keeping up with the execution speed of non-persistent languages is a fundamental goal in persistent language architecture. As the following discussion illustrates, designers of persistent languages obtain required performance by giving up security.

If J is non-persistent, then the following increment statement executes in one microsecond or less:

```
J = J + 1;
```

On the other hand, if J is persistent, then this statement becomes an update. If the storage system runs in a different address space from the user program, then an address space switch must occur to process this command. Because of the address space switch, the command will run perhaps two to three orders of magnitude slower than in the non-persistent case. Such a performance hit is unacceptable to users, which is why persistent storage systems are designed to execute in the same address space as the user program, as shown in Figure 1.3. Note that the separate functionality shown in Figure 1.2 is collapsed into a single address space in Figure 1.3.

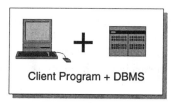

Client Program + DBMS

FIGURE 1.3   The Architecture of Persistent Languages

Avoiding an address space change provides much higher performance. However, it has one dramatic side effect. A malicious program can use operating system calls to read and write any data that the storage system is capable of reading or writing. Because read and write calls for both the program and the storage system run in the same address space, the operating system cannot distinguish them from a security perspective. As a result, any user program can read and write the entire database by going around the persistent storage system and dealing directly with the operating system. Clearly, no prudent database administrator ever stores sensitive material such as employee salaries in such an unsecured environment. For many applications that fit in the lower-right quadrant of the matrix, such as ECAD programs, this trade-off of security for speed is acceptable.

Why doesn't this discussion apply to relational DBMSs? There is a crucial difference between a persistent language world and a relational DBMS. In the persistent language world, updates are very "lightweight," that is, they take very small amounts of time. The useful work in the example update

```
J = J + 1;
```

takes at most one microsecond. As a result, an address space switch requires orders of magnitude more time and is therefore prohibitively costly to implement on each update. In the relational world, updates involve locating and then modifying one or more records through a B-tree, which requires a substantial path length. Thus, updates are much "heavier" than in the persistent language world. The following SQL statement is a typical heavyweight update:

```
update emp
set salary = salary * 1.1
where startdate > '1980-12-31';
```

As a result, expressing updates in a low-level language such as C++ is fundamentally different than in a high-level notation such as SQL. In C++ or any other third-generation programming language, updates are fundamentally lightweight, that is, they modify a single storage location. In this environment, an address space switch per update is prohibitive. In contrast, SQL updates are much heavier and an address space crossing entailed by the client-server architecture is a less severe penalty.

The Players in the O Vendor Market: Still a Market Niche

Systems that focus on providing tight integration with a programming language and high performance for updates to persistent variables are known as object-oriented DBMSs. Such products are available for C++ and Smalltalk, from a collection of object-oriented DBMS vendors, such as Objectivity, Object Design, Ontologic, Versant, Servio, O2, and Matisse. This group is known collectively as the "O vendors."

Because they focus on programming language access to complex data, these systems can be placed in the lower-right quadrant of the matrix. In aggregate, the O vendors are generating about $80 million per year in revenue and are growing at nearly 50% per year. But this business remains a market niche in the database world and is about two orders of magnitude smaller than annual revenues for the relational vendors.

Your DBMS choices here are quite easy. If you have an application in the lower-right quadrant, choose a vendor of a persistent language for your chosen programming language. That vendor is committed to the performance and features required in this corner of the matrix.

At this point, you might be wondering, "What happens if I have a lower-right quadrant application and I run it on a relational DBMS?" The answer is simple. Instead of being able to state

```
J = J + 1;
```

you have to express this command in SQL to a relational database. Because the C++ type system is much more elaborate than that of SQL, you have to simulate the C++ type system in SQL. This simulation is time-consuming to write and requires you to manually map your C++ variables into SQL on reads and writes. Moreover, you perform a heavyweight client-server address space crossing on most commands. As a result, the application runs very slowly. Put more directly, using a DBMS designed for one kind of application in a very different environment can result in serious problems. Relational systems essentially don't work on lower-right quadrant problems.

The opposite question also bears asking: "What happens if I have an upper-left quadrant problem and I run it on an object-oriented DBMS?" Again, the resulting application is not at all graceful. Specifically, most O vendors have limited SQL, and several do not support updates at all from SQL. So, you have to drop into C++ to express your transactions, which results in a great deal more code. In addition, the products of the O vendors are typically not optimized for supporting 50 or 100 concurrent updating users, and consequently performance tends to be very poor. Object-oriented DBMSs don't work well on upper-left quadrant problems. Using any DBMS designed for one kind of application in a very different environment results in a disaster.

1.5   *Quadrant 4: Complex Data with Queries*

The next application is query-oriented and requires complex data, making it representative of the upper-right quadrant of the matrix. The State of California Department of Water Resources (DWR) manages most of the waterways and irrigation canals in California, as well as a collection of aqueducts, including the massive state water project. To document their facilities, DWR maintains a library of 35-mm slides. Over time this library has grown to 500,000 slides and is accessed many times a day by DWR employees and others.

Typically, a client requests a picture by content. For example, an employee might need a picture of "the big lift," the massive pumping station that lifts northern California water over the Tehachapi Mountains into southern California. Other requests might include San Francisco Bay at sunset; Lake Cachuma, a Santa Barbara County reservoir with a low water level; or an endangered species of water fowl on the banks of the American River.

DWR has found that it is very difficult to find slides by content. Indexing all the slides according to a predefined collection of concepts is a prohibitively expensive job. Moreover, the concepts in which clients are interested change over time. For example, interest in low reservoir levels grew when California's most recent drought began seven years ago.

DWR has a written caption about each slide, for example, "picture of Auburn Dam taken during scaffold construction." DWR also maintains a fairly primitive system that can identify slides from specified keywords. This keyword system is not operating very well because many concepts of interest are not mentioned in the caption and therefore are difficult to retrieve.

As a result, DWR is scanning the entire slide collection into digital form and is in the process of constructing the following database:

```
create table slides (
                      id          int,
                      date        date,
                      caption     document,
                      picture     photo_CD_image);

create table landmarks (
                      name        varchar (30),
                      location     point);
```

Each slide has an identifier, the date it was taken, a caption, and the digitized bits in Kodak Photo-CD format. Photo-CD format is a collection of five images ranging from a 128 byte × 192 byte thumbnail to the full 2 kbyte × 3 kbyte color image. DWR has digitized about 40,000 images and is well on its way to building a database, which will be around three terabytes in size (Ogle and Stonebraker 1995).

DWR is very interested in classifying their images electronically. As noted above, classifying them by hand is not practical. One of the attributes DWR wishes to capture is the geographic location of each slide. DWR's technique for accomplishing this geo-registration involves a public domain spatial database from the U.S. Geologic Survey. Specifically, they have the names of all landmarks that appear on any topographic map of California, along with the map location of the landmark. This is the table landmarks mentioned above. They propose to examine the caption for each slide to determine whether it contains the name of a landmark. If it does, the location of the landmark is a good guess for the geographic position of the slide.

In addition, DWR is also interested in writing image-understanding programs that will inspect an image and ascertain attributes of the image. For example, you can find a sunset in this particular slide library by looking for orange at the top of the picture. Low water in a reservoir entails looking for a blue object surrounded by a brown ring. Many attributes of a picture in which DWR has an interest can be found using fairly mundane pattern-matching techniques. Of course, some attributes are much more difficult, such as ascertaining whether the picture contains an endangered species. These harder attributes will have to wait for advances in pattern recognition.

The schema mentioned above contains a caption field that is a short document, a picture field that is a Photo-CD image, and a location field that is of type geographic point. Because it has complex data, this example belongs on the right side of the matrix on page 2.

Moreover, the clients of DWR's database will submit ad hoc inquiries. One such inquiry is to find a sunset picture taken within 20 miles of Sacramento. Clients want a friendly interface that assists them in stating the following SQL query:

```
select id
from slides P, landmarks L, landmarks S
where sunset (P.picture) and
contains (P.caption, L.name) and
L.location || S.location and
S.name = 'Sacramento';
```

Here are the steps involved in making the query:

1. Find the geographic location of Sacramento (S.location) in the landmarks table.

2. Then, find other landmarks (L.location) that are within 20 miles of S.location. || is a user-defined operator defined for two operands, each of type point, that returns true if the two points are within 20 miles of each other. This is the set of landmarks that can be used to ascertain if any appear in a caption of a picture.

3. The function *contains* is a user-defined function that accepts two arguments, a document and a keyword, and determines whether the keyword appears in the document. The function *contains* yields the set of pictures that are candidates for the result of the query.

4. Lastly, *sunset* is a second user-defined function that examines the bits in an image to see whether they have orange at the top. The net result of the query is the one desired by the client.

Obviously, this application entails "query mostly" on complex data. It is an example of an upper-right quadrant application. Here are the basic requirements for upper-right quadrant applications:

Query Language. Notice in the example query about Sacramento sunsets that there are four clauses in the predicate of the query. The first contains a user-defined function, *sunset*, and is thereby not in SQL-92. The second clause has a user-defined function *contains*. The third clause contains a user-defined operator, ||, which is not in SQL-92. Only the last clause is expressible in SQL-92. Upper-right quadrant applications require a query language that allows at least user-defined functions and operators. The first standard version of SQL with these capabilities is SQL-3, now in draft form. Any SQL-2 DBMS is useless on this application, because three of the four clauses cannot be expressed in SQL-2.

Client Tools. DWR wants its application to display a map of the state of California. Then, the user can circle with a pointing device the area of the state that is of interest. On output, the user wants to see a map of Sacramento County with a thumbnail of each image positioned at its geographic location. With the ability to "pan" over the county, the user could examine thumbnails of interest. In addition, the user wants the capability to "zoom" into given areas to obtain the higher resolution images stored in Photo-CD objects. Such a "pan and zoom" interface is typical of scientific visualization products such as Khoros (Rasure and Young 1992), Data Explorer (Lucas et al. 1992) and AVS (Upson 1989). DWR also wants a visualization system fully integrated with the DBMS. Notice that a standard 4GL is nearly useless on this application; there is not a business form in sight.

Performance. The user requires goal performance for queries such as the Sacramento *sunset* query. These are typically decision support queries with significant predicates in them. To perform well in this environment, a collection of optimizations are required. For example, the *sunset* function often consumes 100 million or more instructions. As such, if the query optimizer ever sees a clause of the form

```
where sunset (image) and date < '1985-01-01'
```

it should perform the second clause first, thereby eliminating some of the images. Only if there is nothing else to do should the *sunset* function be evaluated. Being smart about functions that are expensive to compute is a requirement in the upper-right quadrant. Moreover, if many queries use the *sunset* function, then it will be desirable to precompute its value for every image. Therefore, you would execute the function once per image in the database, rather than once per query wanting sunsets. Automatically supporting precomputation on image insertions and updates is a very useful optimization tactic. Lastly, in order to find the landmarks within 20 miles of Sacramento, an efficient "point in circle" query is needed. Such two-dimensional queries cannot be accelerated by B-tree indexes, which are one-dimensional access methods. Traditional access methods (B-trees and hashing) are worthless on these sorts of clauses. To accelerate such spatial clauses, you need a spatial access method, such as a grid file (Nievergelt et al. 1984), R-tree (Gutman 1984), or K-D-B tree (Robinson 1981). A DBMS capable of handling these kinds of queries must either have such "object-specific access methods" or allow a sufficiently wise user or system integrator to add an access method. Obviously, the best technical answer is both.

Notice that optimizing TPC-C is irrelevant to this application. There are essentially no transaction processing applications in the upper-right quadrant.

Security/Architecture. Because upper-right quadrant applications require security, the DBMS should run in a client-server architecture as noted in Figure 1.2 on page 5. Security is rarely tradable for performance in this environment. Moreover, since this is a complex query world, the commands are very "heavy," and the performance win to relinquishing security is much less dramatic than in the lower-right quadrant.

The Players in the Object-Relational DBMS Market

DBMSs that support a dialect of SQL-3, include non-traditional tools, and optimize for complex SQL-3 queries are called object-relational DBMSs. They are relational in nature because they support SQL; they are object-oriented in nature because they support complex data. In essence they are a marriage of the SQL from the relational world and the modeling primitives from the object world. DBMSs that have these criteria are a fit for the upper-right corner of the matrix.

Object-relational DBMS vendors include Illustra, Omniscience, UniSQL, and Hewlett-Packard (with their Odapter for Oracle, also packaged for HP's own Allbase/SQL as Open ODB).

1.6   *The DBMS Matrix Summarized*

In addition to simple file systems, there are three different kinds of DBMSs, each with its own focus on a particular segment of the marketplace. All of these four segments require very different query languages and tools and are optimized with different kinds of engine enhancements. Also, the requirements for security differ among the segments. In effect, the marketers of each kind of engine have carefully "scoped out" a segment of the marketplace and then optimized for that segment.

As already noted, an SQL-92 system is not suited to solving an upper-right quadrant problem, because SQL-92 cannot express the user's queries. Queries must be executed in a user program, which generates a lot of work for the user. In addition, if *sunset* is executed in user space, then a very large image will be transmitted over a client-server connection from server space to client space. This will cause a severe performance problem. A relational DBMS will handle upper-right quadrant problems very awkwardly, very slowly, and very expensively.

Similarly, a persistent language often does not have a rich enough query language capability for expressing user queries. User queries must be expressed as a C++ program, a tedious and convoluted proposition.

If you have a lower-right quadrant problem, it makes no sense to use a relational DBMS to solve it as noted earlier. SQL is simply the wrong kind of interface. Similarly, you would not use an SQL-3 system for exactly the same reasons. An object-relational DBMS is not the answer to a lower-right quadrant problem.

Lastly, if you have an upper-left quadrant problem, then you can certainly use an object-relational DBMS to solve it. Clearly, SQL-3 is a superset of SQL-92, so you can use an object-relational DBMS to solve an SQL-92 problem. However, object-relational engines have typically not been optimized for transaction processing applications. Expect TPC-C to run slower on object-relational engines.

To summarize, a DBMS oriented toward a specific segment generally doesn't work well on problems in a different segment. Thus, the summary of this section is straightforward:

Classify your problem into one of the four quadrants, and then use a DBMS optimized for the quadrant.

What do you do with an application that fits in more than one quadrant? In effect, you have a composite application that exhibits aspects of more than one of our example applications. This is a complex question. In Chapter 13, an application is discussed that fits in three of the four quadrants; Chapter 14 offers suggestions on how to handle multi-quadrant applications.

1.7   *Why is Object-Relational the Next Great Wave?*

The relational market is about $8 billion per year, while the object-oriented database market is a factor of 100 smaller. The growth rate of both markets is substantial, and I expect their relative size in 10 years to approximately preserve the factor of 100 difference, as illustrated by Figure 1.4. Figure 1.4 also shows that the expected size of the object-relational market is 50% larger than the relational market by the year 2005. There are two dramatic market forces that will cause the object-relational market to dominate, generating the "next great wave."

Force 1: Computerization of New Multimedia Applications. Users are computerizing complex data at an astonishing rate. As noted above, the DWR application is scanning data not currently in electronic form. It is estimated that 85% of the world's useful information is not in electronic form. As significant amounts of this data are captured, they will generate a huge market for primarily upper-right quadrant applications. For example, users are placing information onto the World Wide Web (WWW, or Web) at an incredible rate. Almost all Web applications have the same flavor as the DWR application (which incidentally is a Web one), namely, the wish to publish digital content using the Web as a transport mechanism. Queries are all ad hoc, and typically to multimedia objects. Every Web site has a content cre-

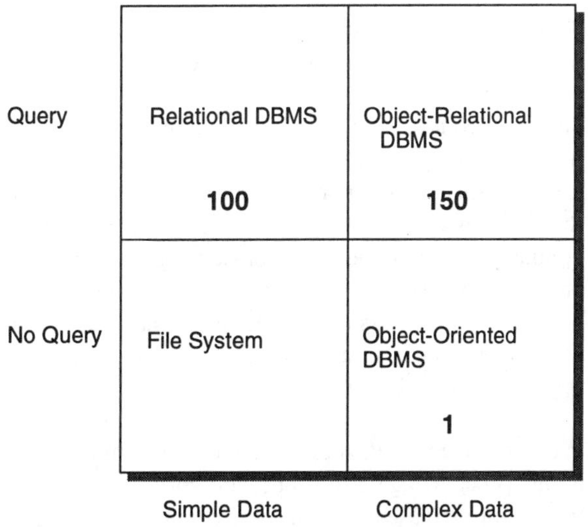

	Simple Data	Complex Data
Query	Relational DBMS **100**	Object-Relational DBMS **150**
No Query	File System	Object-Oriented DBMS **1**

FIGURE 1.4   Relative Size of DBMS Markets in Year 2005

ation, content management, and content access problem, which are all best served by an object-relational DBMS.

The Web, which was virtually non-existent just three years ago, is one example of an explosive new market that will be query-oriented on complex data. A second example where rapid growth is occurring is digital film. Over the next decade conventional film may well disappear as a storage medium for data. This will occur at the high end in medical devices, such as X-ray and ultrasound systems, as well as at the low end in home photography. With a digital camera for snapshots, users generate a digital slide collection on storage in a computer. Then, to browse the collection or form a slide presentation for friends or family, you must run queries against complex data. Digital slide management is an upper-right quadrant application with tens of millions of potential users.

Expect in the next decade that Force 1 alone, the computerization of new multimedia applications, will cause the upper-right quadrant to grow to be approximately equal to the size of the current business data processing market.

Force 2: Business Data Processing Applications Will Move to the Right. A growing need for decision support queries on complex data, hastened by rapidly declining costs in hardware, will cause upper-left quadrant applications to move to the upper-right. For example, consider a typical insurance company that has a customer database and a claims database, presumably implemented as traditional business data processing applications in a relational DBMS. To these applications, the insurance company wants to add the diagram of each accident site, the scanned image of the police report, the picture of the dented car, the (latitude, longitude) of the accident site, and the (latitude, longitude) of each customer's home. Then the company wants to find the 10 most dangerous intersections in each county and charge each customer who lives within one mile of such an intersection a "hazard premium." All of this new data is easily handled by an object-relational DBMS. Over time, expect rightward migration to significantly expand the size of the object-relational DBMS market.

While the scope of the upper-right component is increasing, "technological depreciation" is occurring on the upper-left corner portion of the application. Specifically, the rate of increase in the business data processing load of most upper-left quadrant applications is small, perhaps only 10% per year. For example, the number of customers and number of claims for a typical insurance company are increasing slowly, leading to a slow growth in the business data processing load. At the same time the cost of CPU cycles, disk storage, and main memory are decreasing at almost a factor of two per year. As a result, the cost of executing a given upper-left quadrant workload is declining at the same rate. This makes the business data processing portion of the problem technologically easier, at almost a factor of two per year.

The twin effects of adding an increasingly difficult upper-right quadrant workload to an upper-left application and of hardware advances making the upper-left portion easier and easier will inevitably move upper-left quadrant problems to the right, augmenting the size of the object-relational market.

Forces 1 and 2 combined can be expected to make the object-relational market 1.5 times the size of the relational market. In essence, the major market for DBMSs will move from relational systems to object-relational ones. This "great wave" promises to be at least as significant as the last paradigm shift that occurred from CODASYL to relational systems. Of course, the relational DBMS vendors realize this; their technical options and market strategies are the topics of Chapter 12.

CHAPTER 2   *Characteristic 1: Base Data Type Extension*

This chapter discusses extensible base data types, the first of the four fundamental characteristics of an object-relational DBMS listed in the Preface, and explains why extensible base data types are invaluable for solving upper-right quadrant applications. Three simple example applications in this chapter show how problems that are difficult to deal with in SQL-92 can be easily handled using base type extension. This chapter also explores the mechanism for defining new data types, how to define new operations on data types, and the requirements for a system to be considered fully object-relational in terms of base data type extension.

2.1   *Need for Base Type Extension*

SQL-92 restricts a table column to one of the following data types:

- integer
- floating-point number
- character string, fixed or variable length
- day-time, time interval
- numeric and decimal

Additionally, SQL-92 defines a precise (and hard-coded) collection of functions and operators that are available for each data type. For example, the standard arithmetic and comparison operators are available for integers using the conventional notation. However, it is not possible to easily perform other, more interesting operations such as counting the number of zeros in an integer, or determining if an integer is divisible by some number, because these operations are not defined in SQL-92.

Because SQL's set of data types and operations is limited, many real-world problems are extremely difficult to code and, once coded, perform badly. This section presents three such examples.

Example 1: A Calendar for the Bond Market

The first example is a bond market application. It concerns an actual application developed by an Ingres user. At the time, Ingres (now a division of Computer Associates) had recently released a version of its DBMS that supported date and time as a data type. An Ingres user, who had patiently waited for this new functionality, called the Ingres consulting staff in a rage, saying that Ingres had implemented date and time incorrectly.

Here is a simple version of the user's application and the reason for his agitation. Consider the following (simplified) table that holds a portion of a financial portfolio:

```
create table bonds(
                name            varchar(30),
                rate            float,
                date_bought     date,
                date_sold       date
                interest        float);
```

This table holds a bond portfolio, giving for each bond its name, the interest rate that the bond pays, the date it was purchased, the date it was sold, and the interest to be received. The irate Ingres user was required to compute this interest field. He wished to run the following SQL command:

```
update bond
set interest = rate * (date_sold  -  date_bought)
```

When he ran this command, the Ingres system implemented date subtraction according to the Julian calendar. (Using the Julian calendar, March 15th minus February 15th is 28 days. During leap years it is 29 days, and during double leap years, 30 days). In other words, the exact semantics of the date data type were really Julian date because all the SQL operators on the type utilized this calendar.

Unfortunately, the bond market in the United States does not use the Julian calendar! Instead, a bond holder receives the same amount of interest on a financial bond during each month, regardless of how long the month is. In other words, the monthly coupon is a constant and does not vary with the length of the month. This special Wall Street calendar is integral to the U.S. bond market. (However, it is not universal; most foreign bond markets use the Julian calendar.)

The reason for the user's anger became apparent soon enough. The above SQL statement does not calculate the correct interest because it is operating on the wrong calendar. What the user wanted was a definition of date subtraction that obeyed the calendar used on Wall Street. In fact, according to this calendar, March 15th minus February 15th is always 30 days, and each year is composed of 12 equal-length months, each of 30 days.

The irate user's request was for the data type "bond date" with appropriate operators. From his point of view, Ingres had implemented date incorrectly. More accurately, he wanted bond dates and Ingres had implemented Julian dates. Because the date type operated incorrectly, he could not use the SQL command shown above. Instead, he had to write his own date subtraction function. Then, he had to retrieve the two dates and the interest rate from the database, call his function in user space to perform the correct subtraction, and then put the correct interest back in the database. His lament concerning this solution was twofold:

1. Unacceptable pain for the developer

Every time the user required a calculation on dates, he had to do it in user code. This essentially turned every SQL command into a program. Moreover, the client had to manage the library of bond time functions himself.

The irate user's request to Ingres was, "Why can't I replace the Ingres date subtraction routine with my own?" Of course, Ingres at the time was not architected to allow this functionality, and the answer was that it could not be done. Abstracting this example a little, the user was really asking for the ability to create new data types with their corresponding operators and functions within an SQL context. This capability is called "base type extension."

2. Unacceptable application performance

The user's application was more than a factor of two slower than the corresponding Julian date application. This resulted from the necessity of retrieving data across the client-server boundary and controlling the iteration through the bond table from an application.

Example 2: Alphabetizing Non-ASCII Characters

Consider a version of the traditional emp table, as follows:

```
create table emp(
            name          varchar(30),
            startdate     date,
            salary        float);
```

And, suppose you want to run the following command:

```
select salary
from emp
where name > 'Ly' and name < 'Me'
sort by ascending name;
```

The command requests the salaries of a group of employees within a specific alphabetic range. For a U.S. implementor, this command presents no difficulties. Because the collating sequence for ASCII is the same as for U.S. names, the correct employees will be identified and then sorted into the proper order.

Unfortunately, names in other countries do not necessarily sort according to ASCII. For example, in French, names can have acute accents, grave accents, and circumflexes over certain letters. "E" with an acute accent is not in the ASCII character set. Therefore French names cannot be represented directly in ASCII. If you use a non-printing character for "E" with an acute accent, it will be grouped with the non-printing characters and not the "Es." In other words, the above query will not give the correct answer for French names. The same comment applies for German names, Israeli names, names from most Arabic countries, Japanese names, and Chinese names. In fact, ASCII is only appropriate for names from certain English-speaking countries.

To better support international character strings, facilities were added to SQL-92 to define alternate character sets and alternate collating sequences. These capabilities adequately support many European names. However, most Asian and some European character strings remain problematic. A simple illustration of this issue can be seen by opening the pages of the phone book in Edinburgh, Scotland. There, you will find (for example) that the names McTavish, MacTavish, and M'Tavish are all collated together. These are all variations on the same name, and for sorting purposes, the apostrophe character, "c," and "ac" are considered nulls when they follow an initial "M." Thus, all three variations of the clan's name appear in the phone book along with other names beginning with "MT." This important context sensitivity is not addressed by SQL-92. Simulating the data type "Scottish name" is tedious. You must map "M'," "Mc," and "Mac" into three adjacent ASCII characters. This means remapping all characters so that the sort sequence of the resulting simulation is the proper one for Scottish names.

Of even more significance, the SQL command mentioned above will probably use a B-tree lookup to identify the appropriate employees. B-trees will find all employees who are in collating sequence between "Ly" and "Me." The query execution engine will only work correctly with B-tree indexes if the user maps both "Ly" and "Me" to their simulated values.

Again, writing the simulation is tedious. Moreover, it is slow because every name must be mapped, character by character, when it enters the DBMS and when it leaves the DBMS.

Example 3: A Car Pool

The final example concerns geography. Suppose you want to write a program to manage car pool activity for the employees in a company. You have employee data in an SQL-92 database system, which is illustrated by the following table:

```
create table emp(
                name            varchar(30),
                startdate       date,
                salary          int,
                address         varchar(30),
                city            varchar(30),
                state           char(2),
                zipcode         int);
```

Obviously, candidates for car pools are those who live in the same neighborhood and have a desire to share a ride. Each employee's mailing address is available in the table: the street address, city, state, and zip code. Using the city field in the table emp, the car pool program can try to match prospective riders who live in the same city. If Sam lives in Fresno, then the car pool candidates for Sam can be found by the following query:

```
select name
from emp
where city = 'Fresno';
```

This will not be a very precise implementation because some cities are very large (for example, Los Angeles) and some are very irregular in shape (for example, New York with its five boroughs).

Alternatively, the program could match riders' zip codes. However, zip code regions are rather small for a car pool application and are also quite irregular. With substantial extra effort, you can record some sort of adjacency information for zip codes that allows the program to search neighboring regions.

But the best solution is to record the geographic position of each employee's home, as a (latitude, longitude) point. Then, the car pool program can find neighboring employees as those employees who live within any given distance of each other, where distance is measured "as the crow flies."

With an SQL-92 system, you can add two numbers to the example table as follows:

```
alter table emp add column lat float;
alter table emp add column long float;
```

Here (lat, long) are the coordinates of an employee's home address. Next, suppose you wished to identify prospective car pool candidates for any given employee as those people living close by. ("Close by" will be defined as living within one mile.) The following SQL-92 query identifies the desired car pool candidates for a given employee, Joe:

```
select r.name
from emp j, emp r
where j.name = 'Joe' and
(j.long - r.long) ** 2  + (j.lat - r.lat) ** 2 < 1;
```

There are two (by now very familiar) problems with this SQL-92 statement: unacceptable pain for the developer and unacceptable application performance.

In the unacceptable pain for the developer category, the "close by" calculation is somewhat complex to implement, especially for a novice programmer, and the resulting SQL is not intuitive. As a result, new programmers will take a while to come up to speed on this application.

After the query execution engine finds Joe and returns Joe's longitude and latitude, it must find all employees that satisfy the second clause. This calculation is sufficiently complex that no indexing will be used, and a sequential search of all employees is required. Sequential searching slows performance in almost all cases. Lastly, performing detailed arithmetic in SQL is much slower than the corresponding calculations in a third-generation programming language, such as C. These factors lead to unacceptable performance.

The basic problem here is the necessity of simulating the data type "geographic point" in SQL-92. Because it is not an SQL-92 data type, it must be simulated by using two numbers (lat and long). Moreover, an operation is needed to find points that lie within a designated circle. And, because this operation is not in SQL-92, it must be simulated by coding a collection of numeric operations. This simulation is sufficiently complex that the query optimizer cannot execute the resulting query efficiently.

You have just read three examples that share a common theme. They all entail data types and operations that are not in SQL-92. In each of these examples, simulating the required functionality in SQL-92 is painfully difficult to code and results in very poor performance.

The remainder of this chapter discusses extensible base types, a solution to both of these problems. The examples in the rest of the chapter use the Illustra type extension system syntax. More limited functionality exists in Ingres and DB2/6000 Common Server, as will be noted in Chapter 16.

2.2   *A Better Way: Extensible Data Types*

The extensible data types available in an object-relational DBMS eliminate the awkward type simulations that cause efficiency problems. For example, the car pool application described earlier in this chapter can be neatly streamlined with extensible data types, as shown below.

Illustra packages a collection of data types, their associated functions and operators, and access methods into "DataBlade modules" (using the metaphor that the DBMS is a razor into which DataBlade modules are inserted). One of the DataBlade modules supports 2-D geometric objects and contains a 2-D point data type, in addition to lines, polygons, ellipses, circles, and many other 2-D types. (Of course users are also free to construct their own types and functions.) By using the point data type, you can add the following attribute to the car pool application's emp table:

```
alter table emp add column location point;
```

The point data type encodes a 2-D point by recording a pair of floating-point numbers. Included in the 2-D Spatial DataBlade module is a function that determines the distance from one point to another and one that constructs a circle, given a point as the center and a number for the radius. With the types and functions in the Illustra 2-D DataBlade module, you can recode the car pool query as follows:

```
select r.name
from emp j, emp r
where j.name = 'Joe' and
distance (j.location, r.location) < 1;
```

This query is more understandable and more accessible to a novice programmer than the SQL-92 statement discussed earlier. Moreover, instead of a B-tree as an access method, the Illustra 2-D Spatial DataBlade module uses an R-tree (Gutman 1984), which is much more efficient for this application. All told, query execution for this application is dramatically faster than that for an SQL-92 system. Similar improvements in performance and development time are available in the other two example applications by using extensible base data types.

The next section in this chapter describes how you can create your own base data types. (For query optimization, there are steps a user needs to take when defining a new type. This discussion is deferred until Chapter 10.)

Creation of Base Data Types

In an object-relational DBMS, you create a new base data type by indicating the name of the type, storage information about the type, and routines to convert the data type from ASCII and back. Here is an example of the creation of a new base data type, called mytype_t:

```
create type mytype_t (
                internallength = 8,
                input  = mytypeInput,
                output = mytypeOutput);
```

Internallength indicates that eight bytes are to be allocated to store instances of the type. For example, if a table my_table is constructed that uses the type, mytype_t,

```
create table my_table(
                name         varchar(30),
                some_data    mytype_t);
```

then the system is instructed to leave exactly eight bytes of storage in each row of my_table to store a value for the some_data field.

In addition, the type definition statement includes the names of two functions, *mytypeInput* and *mytypeOutput*, that are called to convert instances of the data type from and to ASCII. The purpose of these functions can be best illustrated by considering an integer example. Suppose an employee, Jane, is assigned a salary of $10,000 as follows:

```
update emp
set salary = 10000
where name = 'Jane';
```

In this SQL statement, notice that the value 10000 is five ASCII characters (1,0,0,0,0) and is 40 bits long. A traditional SQL engine will automatically call the built-in function, ASCII-to-INT, to convert the 40-bit representation into a 32-bit quantity in integer representation for internal storage. Suppose you run another command from an interactive terminal monitor, for example,

```
select salary
from emp
where name = 'Jane';
```

On disk, Jane's salary is stored as a 32-bit integer consisting of 18 leading zeros and then 10011100010000. To display this value on the user's screen, a traditional SQL system will call another built-in function, INT-to-ASCII, to convert the value to an ASCII representation. SQL-92 data types have hard-wired input and output functions to convert between ASCII and the disk representation of the type. In essence, each type has an external (ASCII) representation and an internal (stored) representation.

In an extensible type system, instead of hard-coded routines to move values between internal and external format, the definer of a new type specifies the conversion routines to be used. (This is the purpose of the input and output functions in the SQL **create type** statement in the above example.)

These conversion routines allow wide flexibility on how values are managed. It is possible for the input and output routines to do nothing. If this is the case, the internal and external representations are the same. For example, internal and external representation are the same for the varchar data type, and the conversion routines are not required. It is also possible for the conversion routines to perform an arbitrary transformation. For instance, you can define an encoded data type that encrypts each value before it is stored. The encryption algorithm can be implemented in the input routine while the decryption occurs in the output function.

It is also possible to define data types that include constraints. For example, for determining a pool of potential retirees, it might be required that an employee have an employment start date greater than Jan. 1, 1950 so that the data type startdate cannot have legal values outside of this bound. Conversion routines are a natural place to insert such arbitrary checks on values for the data type. In this case, the input conversion routine can easily perform such integrity checks and reject inappropriate start dates.

Lastly, more exotic transformations are also possible. You can use the input routine to store the actual value external to the DBMS, say in the file system or on a nontraditional storage medium. Then, you can store some sort of identifier of the actual value in the allocated space in the table. Simple examples of this methodology include "file as a data type" or "moniker as a data type."

At this point, you might be wondering what the relationship is between domains in a relational system and data types in an object-relational system. In an object-relational system, a data type is defined as a stored representation of a particular kind of information together with the appropriate operators and functions for the information. In other words, a data type is both information and operations. In contrast, the relational notion of a domain includes only the stored representation, and there is no behavior associated with a domain.

The flexibility of object-relational type systems makes them an extremely powerful means to model complex database applications. But by themselves, new data types are not very useful unless you can perform operations on instances of the type. The rest of this chapter provides the remaining piece of the extensible data type puzzle—how you can define operations on the type.

2.3   *User-Defined Functions and Operators*

In a traditional SQL system, arithmetic and comparison operators are available for arithmetic data types. For user-defined types, you must be able to add type-specific operations. This requires an extension capability for functions and operators.

In an object-relational DBMS, you can write functions in either SQL or a general-purpose third-generation programming language such as C and then register them with the system. Over time, it will be possible to write functions in a variety of languages such as Visual Basic, Java, and Tcl. To register a function, you must indicate the name for the function, its arguments, its return type, and the code to execute for the function. The format of this command is

```
create  function function-name (type_name-1, ..., type_name-k)
              returns        type-name as
              (file-name or SQL expression);
```

For example, you can specify a very simple *hourly_pay* function that divides an annual salary by the 2000 hours in a year:

```
create function hourly_pay (int)
          returns float as
          select ($1/2000);
```

Here the function *hourly_pay* accepts an integer argument and returns a float. The actual computation is expressed in SQL as the argument, $1, which is presumably the annual salary of an employee, divided by 2000 (the number of hours worked in a year). The function *hourly_pay* can now be freely used in any query, for example,

```
select name
from emp
where hourly_pay(salary) > 12.50
```

At runtime, an object-relational server substitutes the definition of the function into the query to produce the following query, which is actually executed:

```
select name
from emp
where salary/2000 > 12.50;
```

Thus, functions written in SQL are *unwound* during query execution. Use of such functions simplifies user queries and results in no performance degradation. Here is a slightly more complex function, *salary_compare_Joe*, that returns the difference between a given employee's salary and that of Joe:

```
create function salary_compare_Joe (int)
    returns int
    as    select $1 - salary
          from emp
          where name = 'Joe';
```

Again, you can freely use *salary_compare_Joe* in a query, for example:

```
select salary_compare_Joe (e.salary)
from emp e
where e.name = 'Fred';
```

Like all SQL functions, this one is unwound during query execution to

```
select f.salary - e.salary
from emp e, emp f
where e.name = 'Fred' and
f.name = 'Joe';
```

You can also write user-defined functions in C. Here is a more complex function, *vesting*, that determines the percentage of an employee's stock option that has vested. The following pseudocode specifies monthly vesting over five years. (Note that the actual vesting calculation does not kick in until the employee has worked for one year.)

```
float vesting (startdate)
{
compute result = current_date - startdate;
convert result to months;
if result < 12 months return 0;
else return result/60;
}
```

If the above function is compiled and the executable result stored in the file foo, you can then register this function using the following statement:

```
create function vesting (date)
returns float
as external name 'foo'
language C;
```

With this definition in place, you can again use the function in an SQL statement:

```
select name
from emp
where vesting(startdate) > 0.6;
```

Execution of user-defined functions written in C differs from the execution of those written in SQL. C functions are "opaque" and cannot be unwound by the execution engine. Instead, the C function must be called by the execution engine during query processing. In fact, the Illustra server dynamically loads the code for the function during execution in either the server or the client process. Also, there are other pieces of information specified at function registration time that deal with query processing. Discussion of these is deferred to Chapter 10.

Notice that traditional SQL supports a considerable collection of operators. For example, the comparison operators { <, <=, =, >=, >, <>} are defined for both integers and floats. Syntactically, an operator is a function with two arguments and the operator name appears in between its arguments. For example, consider the query

```
select name
from emp
where salary > 10000;
```

Here, > takes two integers as arguments and returns a Boolean. The above query is equivalent to

```
select name
from emp
where GreaterThan (salary, 10000);
```

Thus, an operator in SQL is really a special kind of function that has two arguments and uses a different notation. A more complex example dealing with a new data type is now presented. Return now to the car pool example for Joe, first introduced on page 25:

```
select r.name
from emp, emp r
where emp.name = 'Joe' and
distance (emp.location, r.location) < 1;
```

This query can also be expressed as

```
select r.name
from emp, emp r
where emp.name = 'Joe' and
contained (r.location, circle (emp.location, 1));
```

Here, a circle of radius one mile around a center of Joe's location is first constructed. Then, the outer function, *contained*, finds the points that are inside this circle. The outer function takes two arguments, a point and a circle, and returns a Boolean. Notationally, the function is to the left of its arguments, which are delineated using parentheses. Alternatively, the following operator notation could be used:

```
select r.name
from emp, emp r
where emp.name = 'Joe' and
r.location << circle (emp.location, 1);
```

Here, the token << represents the operator notation corresponding to the function *contained*.

Support for User-Defined Operators

Traditional SQL has a fairly rich set of operators as well as a few functions, for example, *sum* and *count*. You saw in the discussion above how to define functions for new data types. How are user-defined operators supported?

In the Illustra system, you use the **create operator** command to register operators, namely,

```
create operator
binding opr-name
to function-name;
```

This specification allows you to use any token for an operator and then bind it to a specific function. Moreover, the token need not be the same name used for the function specification.

This section concludes by indicating how functions and operators relate to database procedures in relational systems. Basically, a database procedure is a collection of SQL statements with other statements interspersed in a vendor-proprietary programming language. Database procedures were pioneered by Britton-Lee as a performance enhancement for transaction processing applications and subsequently adopted by all major relational vendors. Using traditional SQL, the TPL-C bench-mark is five commands that result in 10 messages between client and server processes (Gray 1993). With a database procedure defined on the server, the user merely executes it and only two messages are required.

Note that a database procedure is merely a user-defined function written in a proprietary language that accepts SQL-92 data types as arguments. Unfortunately, the only operation available for database procedures is to execute them. In contrast to user-defined functions, they cannot appear in the middle of SQL commands. Thus, they should be considered "brain-dead" user-defined functions.

2.4   *Fully Object-Relational Type Extension*

The previous sections discussed the concepts of user-defined types and their associated functions and operators. This section suggests specific features that a system must support in order to be *fully* object-relational in terms of base type extension.

Feature 1: Dynamic Linking

A good object-relational DBMS dynamically links user-defined functions so that they are not in the DBMS address space until they are needed. The following paragraphs explain why this requirement is so important. In a good object-relational DBMS, it must be easy for the user to add a new data type, operator, or function. Having to take the system down to install a new type or function means that installation must be scheduled sometimes days in advance with a central system administrator. As a result, static linking can become highly inconvenient for users.

User-defined functions are often refined over time by the developer. When this occurs, the function must be redefined to the DBMS. If the DBMS performs static linking of functions, then the DBMS must be taken down, relinked, and reinstalled. Taking the system down and rebuilding it is a heavy penalty to pay for an algorithm improvement.

A typical object-relational DBMS installation is expected to have a substantial number of user-defined functions. If they are statically linked in the DBMS address space at the time the DBMS is installed, then the "footprint" of the DBMS is enormous. It is plausible for the size of the DBMS to increase by a factor of five or even 10, as a result of static linking of a big library of user-defined functions. This is especially true for pattern recognition and image understanding functions, which are both numerous and large. In most operating systems there is additional operating system overhead and paging activity as the footprint increases. And, if the footprint becomes too large, some operating systems will actually "choke."

Thus, for reasons that range from operating system performance to user convenience, a good object-relational DBMS dynamically links user-defined functions.

Feature 2: Client or Server Activation

A second required feature concerns where the function is activated. An obvious option is to activate a function on the server in the same address space as the DBMS. Consider the function, *contained*, from the above example (page 33). In this case, it must be called for a collection of possibly qualifying emp records and have passed an instance of a point and a circle. If the function is activated in the same process as the DBMS, then this activation is a local procedure call and there is little overhead to the call.

On the other hand, if the function runs in a different address space or on a different machine, then a remote procedure call (RPC) must be used and the arguments copied to a different address space. The overhead of a remote procedure call is substantial, and performance will degrade significantly in this case. Simply put, if the cost of executing a function and/or copying the arguments is not large when compared with the cost of an RPC, then the RPC will add significant overhead. If the function is called many times, then performance will degrade badly.

In contrast, consider a function that is very expensive to compute, such as the *sunset* function mentioned in Chapter 1. This function may consume 100 million or more CPU cycles per invocation, and the cost of an RPC is lost in the noise relative to function execution. In this case, it is possible to run the function in a separate address space or on a separate machine without disastrous consequences. Moreover, if the server is executing work on behalf of many clients, then it may make sense to activate computationally intensive functions on the user's desktop machine, where large numbers of cycles are readily available. In this case, activation of functions in the address space of the client program is most desirable. There are, however, two additional considerations.

First, there are environments where you might be running a very lightweight client and a very heavyweight server. For example, in video-on-demand applications it is essential to use the cheapest possible computer as a set-top box in order to keep the cost of the box in line for the home customer. Second, the "head-end" machine is a very powerful multiprocessor since it must be able to play multiple video streams simultaneously. In this situation, server-side activation is appropriate for most functions.

The second consideration concerns bandwidth. Return to the *sunset* function introduced in Chapter 1. In this example, the argument to the function may be a

2 kbyte × 3 kbyte color image. Even in compressed form, this may be a megabyte or more in size. If client activation of the *sunset* function is used, then this amount of data will be copied from the server to the client. Depending on the speed and cost of the network connection between the client and the server, this may (or may not) be a serious problem. If the client and server are connected by FDDI or ethernet, then it may be reasonable to pay the cost of a megabyte transmission to move the sunset computation from the server to the client. On the other hand, if the client and server are connected by a lower speed network or even the internet, then client activation will be very problematic.

In conclusion, both server-side and client-side activation can make sense, depending on the particular application. A good object-relational DBMS supports both options. In addition, it may be desirable to switch back and forth as machine speeds, load, and network connectivity change over the life of an application.

Feature 3: Security

With server-side activation there is always the danger that, when users define their own functions, they can accidentally (or intentionally) create a security loophole by reading or writing over database data. It is imperative that a system supporting server-side activation preempt this security risk.

If client-side activation is used, then the function runs in a process with the client's user ID. If server-side activation is used, then the function runs in a process with the DBMS's user ID. Consider a function that is not completely debugged and executes an illegal instruction or makes a jump to a non-existent address. If client-side activation is in place, then the client process will crash, an annoying but contained event. However, if server-side activation is used, then the DBMS process will crash, perhaps disrupting a whole community of users attached to that system.

And if the client crashes, clearly the problem lies with the user's code. However, if the server crashes, then it is not so obvious whether the problem lies with the DBMS or with a user function. This ambiguity is heightened in the case that the function makes a jump that lands in the DBMS code segment, making it even more difficult to isolate the source of the problem. Because the DBMS is not supposed to have control, it will crash, even though the problem actually lies with the user function.

More ominously, consider the case that the function is malicious. With client-side activation, a function can read (and/or destroy) any data that is readable or writable by the client. This, in itself, is a security problem. However, it is far more serious if server-side activation is used. In this case, the function can read and destroy all the data in the database. The reason for this is that all DBMS data is placed in files that are readable and writable by the DBMS process. With server-side activation the database administrator must trust that user-defined functions are not malicious. In many environments this level of trust is not reasonable.

It is imperative that a system supporting server-side activation be able to plug this security loophole, and three techniques are available. First, server-side functions can be activated in a process separate from the DBMS. In this case, the function can be run in an address space with a user identification different from the DBMS. This solves the security problem, but reintroduces the necessity of a remote procedure call and its associated overhead, meaning that although secure, the functions will be slow.

Alternatively, you can use a technique called "firewalls." In this case, a program performs the firewalling by examining the object code of the user's function. If the program finds any jumps in the code or any system calls, it modifies the user's program to be safe. The jumps can be runtime checked with extra code inserted into the user program to ensure that they do not go outside the region occupied by the code. System calls can be disallowed by causing them to generate runtime exceptions. Using this technique, the resulting program can be guaranteed to have no security problems. Firewalling offers minimal degradation of performance, providing security at a much lower price than running the function in a separate server address space. Further information on firewalling can be obtained from Wahbe et al. (1993).

The final technique would be to write functions in an interpreted language such as Java. Although the performance of interpreted language is much worse than that of compiled languages such as C, there are significant benefits, including bounds checking of each address generated during execution.

Of course, this issue is best solved at the machine architecture level. If a computer architecture supported rings of protection, such as found in Multics (Oganick 1972), then the function could be activated in a different ring from the DBMS. With high-speed ring crossing supported by the hardware, security could be achieved at low overhead without the necessity of custom firewalling software. Unfortunately, this alternative requires the cooperation of hardware designers, which has not been forthcoming to this date.

Feature 4: Callback

Consider once more the *sunset* function from Chapter 1. It is perfectly reasonable for the function to maintain a private database of images that are known sunsets. Then, it can accept an image as an argument and compare it against its database of known images for similarity. In this way, the function computes its result by comparing its argument against a private database. Supporting this functionality requires that user-defined functions be capable of "callback." That is, it must be permissible for them to run queries inside the function. Specifically, a client program can include arbitrary DBMS commands through a client application program interface (API). A user-defined function must be able to use the same interface to invoke DBMS services. Put differently, a function must operate exactly the same way whether it is linked into an application program or invoked by the DBMS as a result of a user issuing an SQL command containing the function.

Note that the SQL command invoked by a function performing callback may in turn have within it a user-defined function also performing callback. This may mean there is an arbitrary nesting of callbacks, and a good object-relational DBMS supports this without getting confused.

Feature 5: User-Defined Access Methods

Return now to the car pool example discussed earlier in this chapter. Suppose you submit the following query:

```
select name
from emp
where location << box ('0,0,1,1');
```

which requests the employees who live inside a rectangle bounded by the origin and the point(1, 1). (As on page 33 the token << represents the operator notation corresponding to the function *contained*.)

An access method is needed here that is appropriate to the data type, point. B-tree is essentially useless in speeding up this query, because it is a one-dimensional access method. Instead, an access method such as an R-tree, grid file, quad tree, or K-D-B-tree is needed. A good object-relational DBMS must allow type definers to add new access methods. Of course, adding an access method must be done by a sophisticated programmer as Chapter 10 explains.

Feature 6: Arbitrary-Length Types

The last required feature is to have user-defined data types without length restrictions. Clearly, there are data types that are fixed length and short (such as location in the emp table). However, there are also data types that are fixed length and long, such as an image type. Furthermore, there are data types that are variable length and long, such as a compressed representation of an image. Obviously, a good object-relational DBMS supports any permutation of {long, short} and {fixed, variable} length.

It is sometimes argued that the BLOBs (binary large objects) present in relational systems adequately support fixed or variable-length data types of arbitrary length. Unfortunately, you can only fetch or store BLOBs. Therefore, because they have no operations available for them, they are not data types.

2.5   *Summary*

This chapter describes how an object-relational DBMS enables users to define data types, functions, and operators. Such extensibility extends the functionality of an object-relational DBMS tremendously by eliminating tedious simulation of new data types and functions necessitated in traditional DBMSs. The payoff is high performance that is obtained relatively easily.

CHAPTER 3   *Examples of Base Type Extension*

This chapter examines examples of base type extension from three distinctly different application areas:

- Geographic information systems (GISs), which provide geographic query capability on data defining two-dimensional spatial objects.
- Digital libraries, which store several formats of image files in image databases.
- Wall Street time series applications required by traders and analysts to examine historical trends on stock data.

By following through these examples, the practical importance of base type extension will become clearer. While each example application manipulates a different kind of data, they all benefit from the power of user-defined base types and customized type libraries.

3.1   *Geographic Information Systems Applications*

GISs are potentially large database systems that store information that is useful for constructing and querying two-dimensional maps. Most governments maintain maps of objects in their jurisdiction. In addition, companies with geographically dispersed assets, such as pipelines and utilities, also maintain a GIS. In order to perform geographic queries, a collection of two-dimensional data types is required. Some of the types you probably need include

- 2-D point, represented as an (X, Y) pair.
- 2-D line, represented as a pair of points, corresponding to each end of the line.
- 2-D polygon, represented by a sequence of points indicating the vertexes of the polygon.
- 2-D path, represented by a sequence of points (in other words, a polygon that is not closed).
- circle, represented by a 2-D point as its center and a numeric radius.
- 2-D rectangle, represented by a pair of points corresponding to the upper-right and lower-left corners.
- 2-D trapezoid, represented by four points of its respective corners.
- 2-D ellipse, represented by two points corresponding to its centers, and a single number indicating the distance from any point on the boundary to both centers.

In addition, 100 or so functions are appropriate for these data types. These include the following:

- *distance(point, point)* returns number.
- *distance(point, line)* returns number.
- *distance(point, polygon)* returns number.
- *distance(line, line)* returns number.
- *distance(line, rectangle)* returns number.

- *contained(point, polygon)* returns Boolean.
- *contained(point, rectangle)* returns Boolean.
- *contained(point, circle)* returns Boolean.

- *overlaps(rectangle, rectangle)* returns Boolean.
- *overlaps(polygon, polygon)* returns Boolean.
- *overlaps(line, polygon)* returns Boolean.
- *overlaps(circle, circle)* returns Boolean.
- *overlaps (circle, polygon)* returns Boolean.

- *make(point, point)* returns rectangle.
- *make(point, point)* returns line.
- *make(point, number)* returns circle.
- *make(point , number)* returns ellipse.

There are many possible representations for two-dimensional spatial objects. This leads to the possibility of a corresponding number of type libraries. To illustrate this point, a second possible representation for 2-D spatial data is discussed next.

Consider storing points as in the above example. Then, instead of representing a line as a pair of points, make it a pair of pointers to points. And similarly, store a polygon as a set of pointers to lines. In this way, points are stored directly, while lines and polygons are stored as collections of pointers. This representation has certain advantages and disadvantages, relative to the first implementation.

The main advantage to storing data using indirection is that if a point is moved, then every line in which it appears is automatically moved. Similarly, every polygon in which these lines appear is automatically adjusted. In other words, automatic data integrity is supported. If, for example, a river changes course, then the polygon on one side of the river will not change unless the one on the other side is also changed. On the other hand, if you store the lines and polygons directly, then each instance of a line containing the point that moves must be found and updated. Moreover, every polygon must be identified and updated. Because this process demands multiple updates, it is error prone.

Obviously, indirection has advantages. However, it also comes with one severe disadvantage, namely performance on queries. For example, to find whether a given point is inside a polygon, the polygon must be constructed out of its lines, which in turn must be constructed from its points. Two levels of pointers must be followed to materialize the polygon so that the correct check can be performed. In contrast, if the polygon is represented directly, then the indirection is not necessary, leading to much better performance.

Thus, representing polygons directly offers higher performance on retrieval in return for the necessity of multiple updates in certain situations. These updates can easily be done automatically using the triggers in modern object-relational DBMSs as discussed in Chapter 7. As a result, data integrity problems can be easily solved.

In summary, better retrieval performance in exchange for worse update performance is available with a direct representation relative to an indirect representation. Therefore, expect type libraries for both representations to have marketplace advocates. But remember that either type library requires a user-defined access method such as an R-tree to perform well, as noted in the previous chapter.

3.2   *Image Type Library Applications*

A second example concerns digital images, such as those in a digital image library. There are a wide variety of formats available for image data, including tiff, gif, group 3 fax, group 4 fax, photoCD and JPEG. All have found acceptance in certain vertical markets, and it is likely that someone would like to store all of them in a DBMS. You could construct a data type for each of the 50 or so popular formats. Alternatively, you can construct a single data type that supports image storage in a variety of formats. The advantage of the latter choice is that a column of a table can store images in more than one format, a desirable feature in "mixed mode" image libraries.

This chapter discusses only a few of the large number of operations required for the image data type. Obviously, you need standard manipulation operations on an image, such as these:

- *rotate(image, angle)* returns image.
- *transpose(image)* returns image.
- *flip(image)* returns image.
- *crop(image, rectangle)* returns image.

Furthermore, it is often desirable to provide contrast enhancement to an image or make it look as if it were created with a different medium, such as oil paints. More sophisticated operations include

- *enhance(image)* returns image.
- *oil_painting(image)* returns image.

Operations on pairs of images are also a requirement:

- *plus(image,image)* returns image.
- *minus(image, image)* returns image.
- *multiply(image, image)* returns image.
- *intersection(image, image)* returns image.
- *union(image, image)* returns image.

Lastly, there are applications where you want to perform content-based retrieval on a collection of images. In general, you want one of two capabilities. First, you might want to find all the images that have a certain semantic characteristic. Chapter 1 has a example of a user who wants to find images that contain sunsets. Second, you might want to find images that are similar to a given image. In this case, you identify an image of interest and then request more images like the indicated one.

In the first case, it could be helpful for the type library to support color analysis by building histograms. The following function is useful for this:

- *histogram(image)* returns relational table.

Other possibly useful functions include edge detection, for example,

- *edge(image)* returns setof (open_polygons).

Using these primitives, you can construct functions to recognize specialized semantic constructs, such as sunsets. In addition, over time, texture and shape information can be included as building blocks.

To find images that are similar to a given image, the following function is required:

- *similarity(image,image)* returns number.

The current technology in this area is to construct a vector of color, shape, edge, and texture characteristics for each image. Then, the *similarity* function finds the distance between pairs of these vectors. Currently, both the vector to be constructed and the distance metric used must be content specific. Therefore, finding similar landscapes is fundamentally different from finding similar portraits or clip art. The performance of commercial products in this area, such as the VIR DataBlade module for Illustra, and a similar type extension for DB2/6000, C/S, is surprisingly good.

3.3   *Time Series Applications*

In Wall Street financial applications, traders and analysts want to examine trends on historical stock data. They have available a database consisting of the closing price of all securities, some 5000 in number, often back to the 1920s. This value is recorded for each trading day for the appropriate exchange involved. Notice that London trading days and New York trading days are not the same. Hence, these applications must be concerned with the integrity of their historical database.

The traditional way of constructing this application is to form a table for each security, such as this table for IBM:

```
create table IBM (
                date       date,
                price      float);
```

Then, if you wished to find the difference between IBM's five-day moving average and its 200-day moving average on July 15, 1995, you would have to write the following program:

```
main ( )
{
find July 16th IBM record;
until 5 records seen
     {
     read previous IBM record;
     update 5 day average;
     update 200 day average;
     }
until 195 records seen
     {
     update 200 day average;
     }
return (5 day average - 200 day average);
}
```

This application requires a custom program as well as a sequential scan of 200 records.

In addition, suppose you wanted to perform the calculation for all stocks. In this case, you must put the above logic inside an outer loop that iterates over all 5000 securities. Now, there are many records examined in 5000 different tables. Moreover, there is no automatic guarantee that prices are recorded only on legal trading days for the appropriate exchange.

This is an application that will benefit tremendously from the use of a type library. Specifically, Illustra has implemented a time series data type that consists of the following information:

- calendar obeyed by the time series
- starting time of the time series
- stride between values (for example, daily or monthly)
- data type(s) of elements (for example, float or polygon)
- legal time series values in order

With this data type, the following stock table can replace the 5000 tables discussed earlier:

```
create table stock(
                name        varchar(30);
                prices      time_series of floats);
```

Here, you have one table, not 5000 tables, and one record per stock, not one record per stock per date. Moreover, only legal values for the calendar utilized can possibly be stored into the stock table, so automatic data integrity is maintained.

Lastly, there are 100 or so legal operations on time series. These include constructing a moving average, extracting a subset of the time series, and aggregating the time series to coarser granularity. With these operations, your query can be formulated as follows:

```
select moving_avg (prices, 5, '1995-07-15') -
         moving_avg (prices, 200, '1995-07-15')
from stock
where name = 'IBM';
```

This query has two main advantages over the previous representation. First, it can be completely expressed in SQL, augmented by the operations in the type library, making it easier for the user to code the functionality. Second, it runs much faster than the previous representation because only one row of one table need be examined. Moreover, the code that walks down the time series is very efficient and has low overhead relative to the code that examines records in a relational system. As a result, performance on most time series queries is one to two orders of magnitude faster than that of a relational system.

In summary, this chapter has shown three examples of type libraries that allow an object-relational engine to be customized for specific vertical applications.

CHAPTER 4

Characteristic 2: Complex Objects

This chapter explores the second basic requirement of object-relational DBMSs, support in SQL for complex objects—objects that are composed of multiple base or user-defined types. The first part of the chapter describes three type constructors: composites, sets, and references. The remainder of the chapter provides extensive examples of the use of each kind of constructor.

4.1 *Type Constructors*

The following three type constructors are basic building blocks for creating complex types in object-relational DBMSs:

- composites (records)
- sets
- references

Composites as a Type Constructor

A *composite* is a data type consisting of a record of values, as shown by the following two examples:

```
create type phone_t (
                area            varchar(3),
                number          varchar(7),
                description     varchar(20));

create type auto_t(
          name        varchar(12),
          year        int,
          license     varchar(7));
```

To construct a composite type, indicate the name of the type along with the name and data type of the constituent pieces. It is acceptable for the pieces of a composite type to be composite types themselves. Stated more formally, if $T_1, \ldots, T_n$ are any data types, then a composite (or record) can be constructed as a data type, consisting of an instance of each of the constituent data types.

You can create a table to hold instances of a composite type, as shown in the following example:

```
create type employee_t(
                name        varchar(30),
                startdate   date,
                salary      int,
                address     varchar(30),
                city        varchar(30),
                state       char(2),
                zipcode     int);

create table emp of type employee_t;
```

The first statement constructs a composite type, employee_t, and then the second statement constructs the table emp to hold instances of this type. Think of tables as containers into which you can place instances of a composite type. Making a clear distinction between types and tables allows you to have many different tables that hold instances of the same type, rather than just one. The advantages of this possibility are discussed in Chapter 6, Inheritance. Notice that the above statements construct the same emp table defined in Chapter 2.

In addition to placing instances of a composite data type into tables, you can also define individual columns of a table as instances of a composite data type. For example, the following table associates a job and the employee who fills it:

```
create table jobs(
                job_desc        varchar(30),
                employee        employee_t);
```

Sets as a Type Constructor

Support of sets as a type constructor is a useful feature for an object-relational DBMS. Formally stated, if T is any type, then setof(T) must also be a data type. Therefore, there is a requirement for both the set of values of a base data type and the set of values of a composite data type.

References as a Type Constructor

It is also useful to support references (pointers) as a type constructor. Thus, if T is a type, then ref(T) must also be a data type that can be used as the type of any column of any table. As a result, the following data types are required:

- reference to a composite
- reference to a set
- reference to a base data type

(In practice, it is not clear that there is a lot of utility to the last data type, and Illustra has chosen not to support it.)

4.2 *Using Type Constructors*

The following sections provide examples of how complex objects can be supported in an object-relational DBMS. Throughout these examples, the following table is used. It contains the name of a department, the floor it is on, the name of its manager, and five other fields that are described later in the chapter:

```
create type dept_t(
                    dname          varchar(30),
                    floor          int,
                    manager        varchar(30),
                    phone          phone_t,
                    autos          setof(auto_t),
                    manager_ref    ref(employee_t),
                    colors         setof(varchar(30)),
                    workers        setof(ref(employee_t)));

create table dept of type dept_t;
```

Manipulating Composites

In the dept table above, phone contains the phone number of the department, which is a composite. In order to manipulate composites, some extensions to standard SQL are required:

1. User-defined functions take arguments or return a result of a composite type.
2. Functions returning a composite type can appear in the from clause of an SQL query.
3. The "cascaded dot notation" references attributes of a composite object.

User-Defined Functions. It is permissible to write functions that take arguments or return results that are composites. For example, you can define a function *sum_digits* that adds up the digits of the phone number of a department and returns an integer. Like any other function, *sum_digits* can be used in any syntactically legal place in an SQL expression. For example, the following SQL finds the sum of the digits in the shoe department phone number:

```
select sum_digits (phone)
from dept
where dname = 'shoe';
```

It is also possible to ask which departments have a sum of digits equal to 50, as follows:

```
select dname
from dept
where sum_digits (phone) = 50;
```

Functions in the From Clause. In traditional SQL, the from clause contains the name of a table, which is a set of composites. Because a composite is a singleton set, it is possible to place a function that returns a composite in the from clause of an SQL command.

Suppose a function is registered that constructs the phone number of the shoe department, as follows:

```
create function shoe_phone
returns phone_t as
          select phone
          from dept
          where dname = 'shoe';
```

The *shoe_phone* function can then be used in an SQL from clause:

```
select number
from shoe_phone()
where area = '510';
```

This query uses the phone information returned from the function, *shoe_phone*, and then returns the seven-digit phone number, if it is in the 510 area code.

Because functions can be written in SQL, it will come as no surprise that you can put a select query instead of a function name into the from clause. Here is an alternative way to solve the above query:

```
select number
from (select phone
         from dept
         where dept = 'shoe')
where area = '510';
```

In this case, the scope of the from clause is a query that returns a composite. Then, the predicate and target list refer to this composite.

Cascaded Dot Notation. The third notation that is useful in the manipulation of composites is the cascaded dot notation (called "path expressions" by some researchers). Consider traditional SQL, which allows attributes of a table to be referenced as

```
table_name.column_name
```

The dot notation references the columns of a table. Similarly, the dot notation can be used to reference the columns in a composite type. So, to find the seven-digit shoe department phone number, you can write

```
select phone.number
from dept
where dname = 'shoe';
```

Here, the scope of the query is the dept table, and the phone column will be retrieved. Because this is a composite, you can use the cascaded dot notation to indicate that you wish only the number field from this composite. The predicate specifies that you are interested only in the shoe department.

The cascaded dot notation can also appear in the qualification. To find the names of departments that have a number in the 510 area code, you can type

```
select dname
from dept
where phone.area = '510';
```

There is another interpretation of the cascaded dot notation. As indicated above, you can think of a composite as having a collection of attributes, addressed as

```
composite_name.attribute_name
```

You can also think of a composite as having a collection of functions, one per attribute. The name of the function is simply the name of the attribute. Typically, you use standard function notation to utilize functions in a query, for example,

```
attribute_name (composite_name)
```

Using this notation, the above query becomes

```
select dname
from dept
where area(phone) = '510';
```

Alternatively, you can use a notation for functions that places the function name to the right of its argument and uses a dot notation, rather than parentheses. This generates

```
select dname
from dept
where phone.area = '510';
```

which is the Illustra-supported notation. Thus, you can think of a composite as a data type with a collection of predefined functions, one per attribute, and addressed with "trailing function" notation. If this interpretation assists you in understanding composites, use it. Otherwise, use the cascaded dot paradigm.

As you can see, the combination of cascaded dot notation, generalization of the from clause, and user-defined functions referencing composites provides an extremely powerful mechanism to manipulate composites in an SQL context.

Manipulating Sets of Composites

Not surprisingly, the same SQL extensions that applied to composites can also be used for sets of composites, for example, the autos attribute of dept.

User-Defined Functions. You must be able to register functions that accept arguments and return results that are sets of composites. For example, suppose a function is written that returns a Boolean if a department has a 1985 automobile. This function, *has85*, can be used in SQL queries, for example,

```
select dname
from dept
where has85(autos);
```

Functions in the From Clause. Suppose a function is registered that constructs the autos in a company's transportation department, as follows:

```
create function transport_autos
returns setof(auto_t) as
    select autos
    from dept
    where dname = 'transportation';
```

The *transport_autos* function can then be used in an SQL from clause:

```
select name
from transport_autos()
where year = 1989;
```

This query uses the year information return from the function, *transport_autos,* and then returns a car's name, if the car is a 1989 model.

Cascaded Dot Notation. Consider the following query:

```
select dname
from dept
where 1985 in autos.year;
```

This query uses the cascaded dot notation to find the departments that have a 1985 automobile. Specifically, autos.year determines a set, and the predicate is true if 1985 occurs in the set. Now consider a more complex query:

```
select dname
from dept
where 1985 in autos.year
and 'Ford' in autos.name
```

This query returns the departments that have a 1985 car and that also have a Ford of any model year.

If you want to find the departments that have a 1985 Ford, you must run a different query:

```
select dname
from dept
where exists
```

```
(select 1
from dept.autos
where year = 1985
and name = 'Ford');
```

A more succinct notation to accomplish the same thing might be something like

```
select dname
from dept
where autos.(year = 1985 and name = 'Ford');
```

In summary, the combination of user-defined functions, cascaded dot notation, and generalized from clauses provides you with the same power for manipulating sets that is available for composites.

Of course, you must always realize that whenever you store a composite or set of composites, there may be multiple copies of the same object. For example, if there is a company phone list table, then each phone number appears once in the dept table and once in the phone directory table, causing an integrity problem in maintaining the list in both locations. Namely, you will have to find and update a department's phone numbers in both places. Therefore, composites and sets of composites are only appropriate for data that

- rarely changes or
- appears only once.

In other cases, use references, the subject of the next section.

Using References

References are a natural substitute for a primary key-foreign key relationship found in traditional SQL systems. In the dept table, the manager column is a foreign key and records the name of the employee who is the manager of the given department. In contrast, manager_ref is another field in the dept table that serves exactly the same purpose, that is, to identify the employee who manages the department. This section explores both implementations in some detail.

Using the foreign key implementation, if you want to find the start date of the shoe department manager, then a join must be performed:

```
select e.startdate
from emp e, dept d
where e.name = d.manager and d.dname = 'shoe';
```

This query is both non-intuitive to write and slow to execute because of the presence of a join.

In addition, you have a foreign key (manager) in the dept table, which must match a primary key (name) in the emp table. Referential integrity in SQL-92 is required to indicate which actions to take to guarantee that the foreign key values in the dept table all appear as primary keys in the emp table. Some action must be taken when

- a department is created with a non-existent manager
- a manager of a department is deleted

In SQL-92 you can specify the following actions to be taken on the insertion:

- refuse the insertion
- allow the insertion but change the manager value to a default value
- allow the insertion but change the manager value to null
- allow the insertion and in addition create a new employee with the name of the manager

Similarly, on a deletion, the following actions are possible:

- refuse the deletion
- allow the deletion but change the manager field to a default value
- allow the deletion but change the manager field to null
- allow the deletion and in addition delete the department

In an object-relational DBMS you could use the above implementation, which is the only one available in a traditional SQL-92 system. However, there is a second option available, using references, which is discussed next.

The Illustra system allows a column in a table to contain a value that is a reference to an instance of a composite type stored in another table in the database. Conceptually, this data type is a pointer to a record of a specific type in a table. In the dept table, manager_ref is a pointer to a record of type employee_t.

References make use of the fact that all Illustra rows have a unique identifier, called an object identifier (OID). An OID is a 64-bit unique identifier that is guaranteed to never change. In fact, an OID is implemented as two quantities, a 24-bit identifier for the table and a 40-bit row identifier within the indicated table.

With this information in mind, note that the actual value stored in the manager_ref field in each row of dept is an OID. In this application, the OID is the one for the manager of this department.

The extensions to SQL required to support references are the following:

1. A specific *deref* function that returns the actual composite, given a reference to it.
2. More generally, support for functions that take arguments or return results of type reference.

Obviously, you can run traditional SQL queries on the dept table, for example,

```
select manager_ref
from dept
where dname = 'shoe';
```

This query returns a reference to an employee, which is the OID of the employee who is the manager of the shoe department. To dereference the pointer in the manager_ref field, the Illustra server provides a *deref* function that takes a reference as an argument and returns a record of the type pointed to. You can use this construct to find the manager of the shoe department:

```
select deref(manager_ref)
from dept
where dname = 'shoe';
```

Deref is an example of a function provided for all reference data types. If you choose to, you can write additional functions. Consider the function *get_mgr* defined as follows:

```
create function get_mgr (varchar)
returns employee_t as
        select deref(manager_ref)
        from emp
        where dept = $1;
```

With this notation, the query can be simplified to

```
select get_mgr ('shoe');
```

You might ask if there is a *ref* function performing the inverse of the *deref* function. Of course, the answer is yes. To get back the OID of the manager, you can code the following statement:

```
select ref(deref(manager_ref))
from dept
where dname = 'shoe';
```

The function *ref* takes an argument that is an instance of the type employee_t and returns a reference (OID) to the instance. A perhaps more realistic use of the *ref* function is to assign a new manager to the shoe department. Using the traditional implementation, you can give the shoe department a new manager named Mark in the following manner:

```
update dept
set manager = 'Mark'
where dname = 'shoe';
```

Using the *ref* function, the same update is coded as follows:

```
update dept
set manager_ref =
     (select ref (emp)
     from emp
     where name = 'Mark')
where dname = 'shoe';
```

Here, *manager_ref* will be assigned a new OID for the shoe department. This OID is constructed by identifying the employee named Mark and then using the *ref* function to find his OID.

The result of the *deref(manager_ref)* function is a composite. You can utilize the cascaded dot notation explored in the previous section to find the birth date of the manager of the shoe department as follows:

```
select deref(manager_ref).birthdate
from dept
where dname = 'shoe';
```

To find both the start date and salary of the manager, type

```
select deref(manager_ref).startdate, deref(manager_ref).salary
from dept
where dname = 'shoe';
```

You have now seen the use of primary key-foreign key relationships as well as a pointer implementation to support representing the manager of a department. You can use a character string (the name of the manager) as a logical pointer, or you can use an OID (reference) as the pointer. Generally, it is somewhat safer to use the reference implementation because an OID is guaranteed to be unique and never change, while an employee's name is not necessarily time invariant.

On the other hand, unlike a character string, OIDs have a format that people cannot easily read. For example, dumping the contents of the manager field in the implementation with an OID pointer reveals data that you cannot quickly decipher.

In short, there are both advantages and disadvantages to using references, and there is no exact answer to the question of when to use references, instead of some other construct.

Using Sets of References

As you read earlier in this chapter, references are pointers to a record of a specific type in a table. If an object-relational DBMS has the notion of sets, it is also appropriate for it to support sets of references. For example, the dept table, defined on page 51, contains a column recording the workers in each department. Because each reference is an OID, it is not surprising that the field workers contains an arbitrarily large collection of OIDs that reference employees who work in the given department. Use *setof(ref(employee_t))* if the field can contain more than you reference. If only one object will be referenced, use *ref(employee_t)*.

Clearly, you can use all the capabilities of set manipulation to deal with sets of references. For example, to find the workers in the shoe department, type

```
select workers
from dept
where dname = 'shoe';
```

This command returns a set of OIDs, which is probably not what you had in mind. To further manipulate the set, you can put it in a from clause:

```
select deref(*)
from (select workers
        from dept
        where dname = 'shoe');
```

Here, you dereference the members of the set to get their actual records. The last step is to indicate you only want employee start dates as follows:

```
select deref(*).startdate
from (select workers
        from dept
        where dname = 'shoe');
```

As you can see, the SQL notation to deal with sets and references can be combined in a straightforward way.

Using Sets of Base Types

The favorite colors for each department appear in the example dept table and are a set of base types (page 51). As with all sets of objects, you must remember that there will be an integrity problem whenever member data is changed. For example, if you decide that magenta is no longer a color and you want it to be called purple, then you have to find all instances of magenta and change them to purple.

How are sets stored? Obviously, the number of members can get arbitrarily large, causing the size of records to also become arbitrarily large. To keep record sizes manageable, one option is to store the members of a set in a disk record separate from the record in which they appear. The OID of this extra record is stored in the actual data record, and there is a level of indirection in the processing of sets. A smarter strategy is to store the set members separately only if the set is larger than a certain threshold. Otherwise, store the set "in line" in the record.

4.3   *Base Types and Complex Objects*

As you have seen, a good object-relational DBMS enables you to extend the system by

1. Defining new base data types and functions.
2. Defining new complex objects and functions, through the type constructors setof, ref, and composite.

Naturally, you are probably wondering why these two mechanisms exist. There are four reasons why a good object-relational DBMS supports two type systems, one consisting of extensible base types and one consisting of complex data types. The reasons revolve around

- naturalness
- encapsulation
- OIDs
- data conversion and ordering

Naturalness

The first reason to support both type systems concerns what is natural for a user to understand. The types phone_t, dept_t, and employee_t are naturally composites, with visible attributes of various types. Moreover, the rows of a table are naturally instances of a composite type. On the other hand, many types are naturally single

quantities, such as Scottish names, positive integers, and images. These are naturally viewed as base types, and it requires some contortion of thought to view them
as composites consisting of a single field of one of the SQL-92 types.

In the last decade three new base types have been added to most commercial relational DBMSs: date, money, and Kanji character string. These additions clearly
demonstrate the need for base type extension. As a result, both complex objects and
base type extension are very natural constructs in specific situations. Thus, it is
desirable to support both possibilities.

Encapsulation

A second reason for both kinds of types concerns encapsulation. Base types are
completely encapsulated. The only way to manipulate a base type is to retrieve it or
execute a function that takes its type as an argument. In contrast, composite objects
are completely transparent. You can see all the fields, and they are readily available
in the query language. Of course, an intermediate position is to allow some fields of
a composite object to be public (visible) and the remainder to be private (encapsulated). This is the approach used by C++.

Obviously, you can change the internal representation of a base type at will. You
need only redefine the input and output functions to store the bits in a different way.
Programs that utilize the type will continue to run correctly. This ability to change
the internal parts of a type is a good argument in favor of encapsulation. In contrast,
visible fields in a complex object cannot be redefined, or all programs that use the
type will stop working. In general, base types are appropriate for encapsulated data,
while complex objects are appropriate for unencapsulated data.

OIDs

In general, complex objects have a system-allocated OID assigned to them, while
base types do not. Therefore, there is a space penalty for using complex types. As
noted earlier, a reference is an OID, and a base type does not have one. Thus, references are available only for complex types.

Conversion and Ordering

Return to the Scottish character string example introduced in Chapter 2. Using base
type extension, you can construct a base data type, Scottish character string, and
then define a collection of comparison operators for the new type. Values can be
stored in a B-tree in ascending order according to the user-defined notion of < (less
than) as will be explained in Chapter 10. A user query such as

```
select salary
from emp
where name > 'Ly' and name < 'Me'
```

is processed by directly using the B-tree index with the predefined comparison operators.

Although Scottish names do not require different external and internal formats, there are many data types, including integers, that do. The input and output functions available for base types naturally support format conversion. As a result, format conversion and user-defined ordering are powerful features of base types.

If base type extension is not supported in a DBMS, then some other mechanism must be available to provide this functionality. The alternate character sets and collating sequences available in SQL-92 are an inferior solution particularized to a specific kind of data. Therefore, specification of type semantics in the underlying language is not attractive.

Alternatively, it is plausible to define input and output functions as well as operators for complex objects. Then, you could cast a Scottish name to a complex object to get the required functionality. This seems much less natural than supporting base type extension. Format conversion, indexing, and user-defined operators seem best handled at the base type level.

4.4 *Summary*

You have seen several reasons why a good object-relational DBMS must support both base types and complex objects. To conclude the chapter, this section presents the features that a system needs to support in order to be considered fully object-relational in terms of complex types.

Feature 1: A rich collection of complex types must be supported.

At a minimum, the type constructors "composite," "set of," and "reference" must be supported. Without these three mechanisms, there will be problems that will be very difficult to express. For example, if a DBMS does not support sets of base types, then the colors column in the dept table (defined on page 51) cannot be expressed as

```
colors    setof(varchar(30)),
```

Instead, you have to create a composite type, color_t, containing a record with one column, color, as follows:

```
create type color_t (
        color   varchar(30));
```

Then, colors can be contained in the dept table through the following, rather unnatural, construct:

```
colors    setof (color_t),
```

Also, depending on the implementation of sets of composites, the second implementation may have worse performance than the first one. The best solution is to support all the needed sets and references.

Feature 2: Functions must be available for all complex types and have the required properties of functions mentioned in Chapter 2.

Clearly, you cannot do much with complex types unless there are user-defined functions available. And in order to be useful, these must include the *ref* and *deref* functions, explored in this chapter. The same reasons for having required properties for functions on base types hold for complex types.

Feature 3: There can be no limit on the size of complex types.

Obviously, sets can be unbounded in size. Any restriction on the number of members of a set or on the amount of space they can consume will be an obvious hardship.

Feature 4: SQL support for complex types is required.

For composites, the cascaded dot notation is required to reference the member attributes of the composite. In addition, functions that return a set, including ones written in SQL, must be able to appear in SQL anywhere that a table can appear in an SQL query.

CHAPTER 5

Other Type Constructors?

Chapter 4 discussed the type constructors, "composite," "set of," and "reference to." You will learn in this chapter that there are many more possible type constructors, including

- list
- stack
- queue
- array
- insertable array

Compared with the three major type constructors discussed in Chapter 4, these constructors have more limited usefulness. However, in specific applications they can be very useful.

The first four constructors listed here are popular type constructors from programming languages and have the obvious interpretation. The last constructor, insertable array, is a specialized kind of array. In a normal array, you can assign a value to any array element, and inserting a value in the middle of an array does not change its length. In contrast, consider the needs of a text editor, which might require that the lines in a document be an array of variable-length strings. When an insert in the middle of this array is performed, all the lines subsequent to the insertion point need to be "pushed down one," so that all their line numbers are augmented. An insertable array is a data structure with this property.

Although most object-relational vendors have focused their initial attention on the type constructors discussed in the previous chapter, it is likely that they will expand their offerings over time. To show why additional constructs would enhance the functionality of an object-relational DBMS, this chapter explores the utility of arrays. This discussion explores what is possible, not what exists in current systems.

5.1   A Simple Array Example

As a simple initial example, suppose an employee's salary changes every month. That is, instead of an employee receiving an annual salary in 12 equal installments, the employee can receive a different salary each month. In this case, the salary column in the example employee_t type from Chapter 4 is no longer appropriately an integer. Instead, the column wages, which is an array of integers, can be defined. The revised description of employee_t and its corresponding container, the emp table, is

```
create type employee_t(
                    name            varchar(30),
                    startdate       date,
                    wages           int [12],
                    address         varchar(30),
                    city            varchar(30),
                    state           char(2),
                    zipcode         int);

create table emp of type employee_t;
```

Using standard FORTRAN-style notation, you can define a column of a table to contain an array of values of other types.

With an array data type, retrieving the April salary for all employees in the 94708 zip code is straightforward. Standard array referencing in an SQL statement is used as follows:

```
select wages[4]
from emp
where zipcode = 94708;
```

Contrast this solution with an SQL-92 system where you have to define an auxiliary table of the form

```
create table compensation (
                        name     varchar(30),
                        month    varchar(30),
                        wages    int);
```

Next, the above query requires a join between the compensation table and the emp table, resulting in much poorer performance than the array solution. Specifically, the SQL-92 query is

```
select wages
from compensation
where month = 'April'
and name in
      (select name
      from emp
      where zipcode = 94708);
```

5.2 *Using Arrays to Support Aggregation*

A more realistic use of arrays is to support aggregation, one of several aspects of on-line analytical processing (OLAP). As an illustration, the following sample application uses sales data for a hypothetical company. This company distributes several kinds of products and maintains sales data for each one. Sales data is available by sales region on a monthly basis for the last several years. The company has several different channels by which it distributes its product. Its sales data can readily be organized into the following four-dimensional array:

```
sales (product, time_period, channel, region_number)
```

Naturally enough the company president wishes to browse this sales data. On a two-dimensional computer screen, it is difficult to visualize a four-dimensional array. To assist in his analysis of sales, the president wants to see various combinations of the data displayed. For example, he might want to see

```
sales (product, time_period)
```

with sales aggregated for channel and region. Or, he might wish to see

```
sales (channel, region_number)
```

aggregated for product and time. Other users might want to see this aggregated data for subsets of the array. A sales rep might want to see

```
sales (channel, region_number)
```

only for the eastern portion of the United States. To meet the needs of such applications, a variety of OLAP companies provide efficient storage for array data and high-speed aggregation operations.

Optimizing Array Storage for Aggregation

This section briefly explores why array storage must be optimized for aggregation operations. The naive way to organize a large multidimensional array is "FORTRAN style," with the indices of the array ordered from 1 to n. Then, values of the array are ordered in storage, with the nth index varying most rapidly and the 1st index least rapidly. This organization is illustrated in Figure 5.1, which depicts a two-dimensional array, A. Figure 5.1 also shows that FORTRAN-style arrays result in one matrix row being stored on each disk page (assuming that a disk page holds exactly n array elements). If you are going to read the whole array or if the array is present in main memory, then this is a reasonable representation.

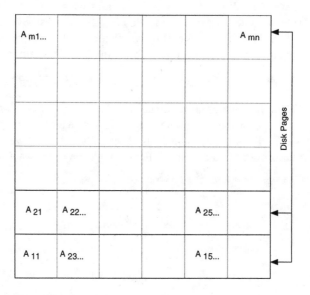

FIGURE 5.1   FORTRAN Representation

However, if you are going to read a "cube" of data from the array that is specified in an ad hoc manner, then FORTRAN representation will not perform well. Because the unit of transfer from disk to main memory is in units of whole pages, not only will the cube be read, but also a lot of extra data that is outside the scope of your query, as shown in Figure 5.2.

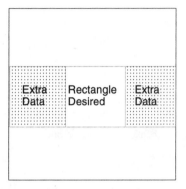

FIGURE 5.2 Performance Problem

To avoid reading extra data with each query, the array should be "chunked," as illustrated in Figure 5.3. Using this methodology, a "stride" is specified for each index of the array and the array is stored on disk in chunks specified as a single stride in each of the indexes. With this organization, it is likely that reading a chunk will entail much less wasted I/O. In the example, the extra data can be seen to be a much smaller set. Several studies (for example, Sarawagi and Stonebraker [1994]) have shown the tactic is generally a very good idea.

Current products implement such functionality in specialized engines. As a result, data must be loaded into such systems, typically by capturing historical data from a transaction processing system. Often the production system uses relational DBMS technology, which leads many users into the architecture indicated in Figure 5.4. Notice that the user must copy data from a relational engine into the second system. In other words, you need two systems, and a clever application program to transfer data from one system to the other.

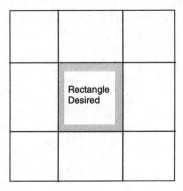

FIGURE 5.3   Chunked Representation

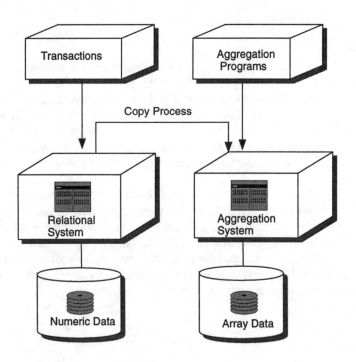

FIGURE 5.4   Traditional Aggregation Operation

In contrast, suppose an object-relational DBMS added the following features to its engine:

1. An array type constructor
2. The appropriate functions and operators on arrays
3. Optimized storage for arrays through chunking

With these extensions, an object-relational DBMS becomes a natural aggregation engine, and the architecture of Figure 5.4 is simplified to that of Figure 5.5. First, the user benefits from using an object-relational DBMS for an aggregation application. Specifically, you can put all of your data in a single DBMS, as shown in Figure 5.5. Moreover, if you wish, for performance reasons, to have array data also appear in a different format for transactional access, then this data replication can be easily supported using object-relational DBMS rules. This will be discussed in Chapter 7.

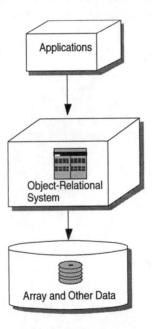

FIGURE 5.5   Object-Relational Support for Aggregation

The user also gets additional functionality. Specifically, an object-relational engine can support arrays of any data type, not just numeric arrays, a limitation that commonly straightjackets specialized systems.

As a result, expect object-relational DBMSs to add additional type constructors over time to provide needed functionality for specific vertical markets. Although arrays were used as the illustration in this chapter, it is highly likely that the same basic argument can be applied to a variety of other type constructors as well.

5.3   *Summary*

A rich set of type constructors along wih a mechanism for user-defined functions are a powerful combination. Arrays plus optimized storage allow an object-relational DBMS to easily integrate OLAP functionality. This integration not only provides you with a more powerful system, but it simplifies administration and eliminates the need to run two systems.

CHAPTER 6 *Characteristic 3:*
Inheritance

The third major characteristic of a good object-relational DBMS is support for inheritance of various characteristics from supertype to subtype. The first section of this chapter concentrates on data inheritance. The next section focuses on function inheritance.

Like base type extension and complex objects, inheritance allows you to define new data types. All three facilities should be carefully used to create schemas that closely model the user's actual problem. Uncontrolled use of any of the facilities can create an explosion of types that may be very difficult to manage.

6.1   *Data Inheritance*

Data inheritance applies only to composite types. Suppose you construct the person_t data type with a single column, name:

```
create type person_t(
                     name          varchar(30));
```

You can now construct two additional data types, employee_t and student_t:

```
create type employee_t (
                        salary      int,
                        startdate   date,
                        address     varchar(30),
                        city        varchar(30),
                        state       varchar(30),
                        zipcode     int)
under            person_t;

create type student_t(
                        gpa         float)
under      person_t;
```

These statements each create a subtype under the supertype person_t. Each of the subtypes inherits all of the data fields from its supertype. The type employee_t inherits name from person_t and then specifies a collection of six additional attributes. Similarly, student_t inherits the same attribute from person_t and then adds a single additional attribute of its own.

A good object-relational DBMS supports multiple inheritance, which means a subtype can inherit data elements from multiple supertypes. And, an inheritance hierarchy can be multiple levels deep. For example, you can construct a student_emp_t data type as follows:

```
create type student_employee_t (
                        percent     float)
under employee_t, student_t;
```

This statement indicates that the type student_emp_t inherits data elements from both student_t and employee_t. Specifically, it inherits the seven elements from employee_t and the two from student_t. Because name appears in both student_t and employee_t, then student_emp_t ends up with a total of nine fields as follows:

- name inherited from person_t
- salary, startdate, address, city, state, zip code inherited from employee_t
- gpa inherited from student_t
- percent, specified in the type declaration

Data inheritance allows you to group composite types into an inheritance hierarchy; the complete type hierarchy for our example is illustrated in Figure 6.1. Types near the bottom of the hierarchy inherit many of their fields from supertypes. This is a good idea because it encourages modularity and consistent reuse of schema components. In addition, inheritance automatically adds all appropriate fields, making it impossible to leave any out. In a system without inheritance, you could inadvertently make mistakes causing data element inconsistencies.

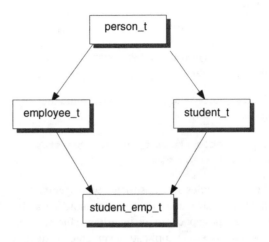

FIGURE 6.1   Example Inheritance Hierarchy

When a data type can inherit its fields from multiple supertypes, there is the possibility of ambiguity. For example, suppose you added the field address to student_t, but assigned it a different meaning than was present in employee_t. Specifically, suppose address in student_t was the complete student address, recorded as a varchar(60). In contrast, the same information is recorded in four fields in employee_t. In this case, student_emp_t has an ambiguity, in that both supertypes have an address field with different meanings.

To deal with this situation, consider taking the simplest possible approach, to disallow the definition of the student_emp_t, which caused the ambiguity to occur. Because of the ambiguity, you must redefine one of the address fields in one of the supertypes before proceeding with the definition of student_emp_t. The alternative is to have ambiguity resolution rules defined by a database administrator. These are invariably complex and difficult for users to understand.

Inheritance only applies to data types. If a table is constructed that is not of a named type, then this table will be of an anonymous type and cannot utilize inheritance. Therefore, you are encouraged to construct types and then assign them to tables rather than merely creating tables. In the former case, you can leverage inheritance; in the latter case, you cannot.

Clearly note that there is no storage associated with types, and tables must be constructed to hold instances of types. For example, you can construct the following four tables:

```
create table person of type person_t;
```

```
create table emp of type employee_t
under person;
```

```
create table student of type student_t
under person;
```

```
create table student_emp of type student_employee_t
under student, emp;
```

These four tables are constructed with specified types. More importantly, they illustrate the construction of a so-called table hierarchy, shown in Figure 6.2. Because the four types appear in the inheritance hierarchy of Figure 6.1, you would naturally expect to construct applications in which instances of each of the four types would be present. Moreover, the opportunity to have the scope of SQL commands be all persons (including those that are employees, students, and student_emps) is important. More generally, it should be possible to reference any table in the table hierarchy of Figure 6.2 and have the scope of the command be the table plus all tables underneath it.

For example, consider the following SQL statement:

```
select name
from emp
where salary = 10000;
```

This statement examines the table emp for employees who earn $10,000; however, it additionally examines all tables under emp in the table hierarchy for other qualifying instances. Thus, the scope of the "from emp" clause is automatically assumed by the Illustra server to be the emp table and all tables that are underneath it in the table hierarchy. If you wish to only examine the emp table, then you would use the following syntax:

```
select name
from only (emp)
where salary = 10000;
```

In this case, only instances from the emp table and not descendent tables are returned.

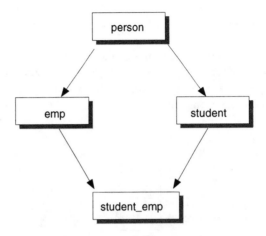

FIGURE 6.2 Example Table Hierarchy

Consider just the person and emp tables and suppose there are P instances in the person table and E instances in the emp table. In this case, the natural implementation is shown in Figure 6.3, namely, two containers, one with P records and one with E records.

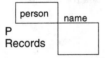

FIGURE 6.3 Illustra Representation

Alternatively, you can store P + E records in the person container, one for each person and employee giving values for their name, and then E records in the emp container giving the additional fields for employees.

This possibility is shown in Figure 6.4. Notice that some mechanism is required to join records in emp to their corresponding records in person, so that all fields of employees can be accessed. For this purpose, you could use a reference to a person record in the emp table.

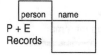

emp	ref(person)	salary	startdate	address	city	state	zip code

E
Records

FIGURE 6.4   Alternative Representation

This latter implementation is advantageous for queries such as the following:

```
select name
from person
```

Here, an execution engine must access the single container person to solve the query, whereas the natural implementation described earlier requires accesses to two containers. In contrast, however, consider the following query:

```
select salary
from only(emp)
where name = 'Joe';
```

In this case, fields in Joe's record appear in both containers, so accesses to both will be required if the alternative implementation is chosen. The natural implementation, however, requires only accesses to the emp container.

A final design is to put all instances in a single large container. This has the disadvantage that indexes are required to find the instances of any given table. A "table per container" model does not require such indexes.

As a result, different implementations of inheritance have different performance properties. You need to understand which option has been selected by the object-relational DBMS you are using, and then try to design databases that are the fastest for that implementation.

Inheritance on types allows a subtype to inherit data elements from supertypes in the inheritance hierarchy. In addition, table hierarchies allow you to scope SQL commands to return results from a table and its descendent tables in a single command.

There is one final point to be explained before leaving this topic. Consider the query:

```
select *
from emp
where salary = 1000;
```

This query retrieves instances from both emp and from student_emp, which have different collections of attributes. It is natural to retrieve only those columns that exist in emp from both tables.

In contrast, you should also be able to retrieve all attributes from both tables, resulting in a "jagged return." This can be accomplished with the following query:

```
select e
from emp e;
```

This feature gives you great power; however, the client program must be prepared to deal with the complexity of a jagged return.

6.2   *Inheritance of Functions*

The inheritance behavior of a user-defined function is determined by its arguments. Specifically, think of attaching to each node in the inheritance hierarchy the names of all functions that have this data type as an argument. Consider, for example, the addition of a new function *overpaid*:

```
create function overpaid (employee_t)
returns    Boolean as
return     $1.salary > (select salary from emp where name = 'Joe');
```

This function takes an instance of the type employee_t as an argument and returns a Boolean to indicate whether the employee is overpaid. In this example, *overpaid* returns true if the instance of employee_t makes a greater salary than that of Joe in the emp table. Figure 6.5 is Figure 6.1 with the addition of function *overpaid*, which is attached to the employee_t node.

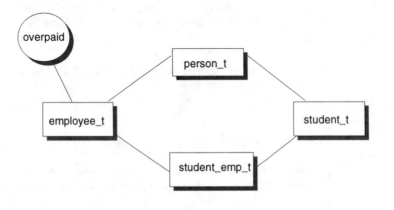

FIGURE 6.5   A Modified Type Hierarchy

Now consider the following query:

```
select e.name
from only (emp)e
where overpaid (e);
```

This query evaluates in the obvious way, using the *overpaid* function just defined. However, consider the query with "only" removed:

```
select e.name
from emp e
where overpaid (e);
```

Here, the scope of the command is the emp table plus the student_emp table. Clearly *overpaid* can be evaluated on the emp table as above. However, suppose there is no function *overpaid* defined on the type student_emp_t. Here, a good object-relational DBMS automatically inherits the function from a supertype. In this case, there is a supertype employee_t, and the *overpaid* function from that data type is used.

If an object-relational DBMS is asked to evaluate a function, and there is no function with the correct name and arguments, then the system searches the type hierarchy for a supertype on which the function is defined with the proper arguments. If one is found, then the system uses this function. In effect, student_emp_t inherits the function *overpaid* from employee_t.

It is permissible to have as many *overpaid* function definitions as are required to implement the user's application. This means if there is a different meaning for student employees being overpaid, then you can add a second *overpaid* function, for example,

```
create function overpaid (student_emp_t)
returns    Boolean as
return     $1.salary >
           (select salary from student_emp where name = 'Bill');
```

This function returns true for those student employees who earn a salary greater than Bill's in the student_emp table. With the addition of this function, the inheritance hierarchy becomes the one shown in Figure 6.6.

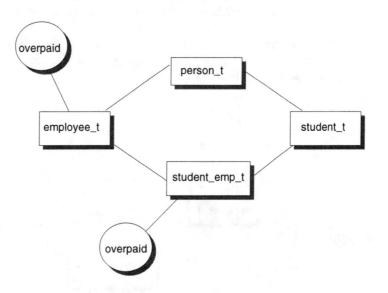

FIGURE 6.6   A Further Modified Type Hierarchy

Now if you run the query

```
select e.name
from emp e
where overpaid (e);
```

an object-relational DBMS uses one *overpaid* on the emp table and the second *overpaid* on the student_emp table. The answer will be the same as if the user had typed the following two queries:

```
select e.name
from only (emp) e
where overpaid (e);

select s.name
from only (student_emp) s
where overpaid (s);
```

This example illustrates that it is permissible to overload the name, *overpaid*, with two different definitions, applying to different data types. At runtime, an object-relational DBMS must utilize the correct function definition. Moreover, there will be queries, such as the one above, for which multiple functions will have to be used in the same query. This concept is also called *polymorphism*, because the function *overpaid* can be applied with different meanings to multiple types.

Consider the deletion of the *overpaid* function on student_emp_t and the definition of a new function *overpaid* for the data type student_t. This results in the inheritance hierarchy of Figure 6.7.

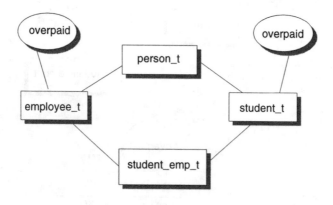

FIGURE 6.7   A Different Modification of the Type Hierarchy

Next, consider the query

```
select s.name
from student_emp s
where overpaid (s);
```

In this case, there is no function *overpaid* defined for the data type student_emp_t. Moreover, there are two possible *overpaid* functions that could be inherited from supertypes, namely the ones for employee_t and student_t. In other words, there is an ambiguity concerning which one to use.

Again, I recommend issuing a runtime error to indicate the ambiguity. It is then your responsibility to resolve the ambiguity by renaming one of the two functions to remove the problem or to write another *overpaid* function that addresses the special case of student employees. Other object-oriented languages address the problem of ambiguity in various ways, all with considerable additional complexity.

In many object-oriented languages user-defined functions are called methods. Conceptually, user-defined functions and methods are exactly the same thing. Therefore, I favor the term *function*.

The following is an alternate explanation of function inheritance in terms of data inheritance. Consider the function, *overpaid*, which takes an instance of employee_t as an argument and returns a Boolean. This function can be thought of in either of two ways.

First, it can be thought of as a function, whose argument is of type employee_t as above. As such, it can be used in queries, for example,

```
select e.name
from emp e
where overpaid(e);
```

This is the interpretation used in this chapter, so far. However, there is a second interpretation of *overpaid*. Specifically, it produces a value for any instance of employee_t. As such, it can be thought of as an additional *virtual* constituent attribute in the employee_t data type. Normal fields in an instance of a composite object are referenced as emp.name, emp.salary, etc. Using this interpretation, *overpaid* can be referenced like any other attribute, for example,

```
select e.name
from emp e
where e.overpaid;
```

These two queries produce the same answer because you can define *overpaid* either as a virtual attribute or as a function. Put differently, you can place the function first in the query and put its argument in parentheses, or you can put the argument first and use the dot notation.

Using the second interpretation, *overpaid* is an attribute of employee_t and therefore can be inherited by descendent nodes in the inheritance hierarchy. As a result, you can think of functions as decorating the inheritance hierarchy and being inherited from supertypes if needed. You can also think of functions as virtual data elements in a type that are inherited from supertypes using standard data inheritance. In the first interpretation function notation is appropriate, while in the second data notation is preferred. In point of fact, the only difference is whether the function precedes its arguments and uses parentheses or whether the argument comes first and the dot notation is used.

So far, composite types have been discussed. However, like composite types, base types can also exist in a supertype-subtype inheritance hierarchy. Therefore, when you create a base type you can specify that it inherits from a base supertype. For example, consider the creation of a new base data type, positive_integers, as follows:

```
create type positive_integers_t(
     internallength = 4,
     input  = pos_in,
     output = pos_out)
under integer;
```

In this case positive_integers_t inherits all the functions from integer that it does not choose to redefine. Of course, they will operate correctly only if positive integers use the same storage representation as integers.

Think of all data types as being grouped into two inheritance hierarchies. The first is a hierarchy of base types, while the second is a hierarchy of composite types. There is no requirement that either hierarchy has a designated root data type, nor is it required that each hierarchy be connected. So, there may be several connected sub-hierarchies that form each of the two hierarchies.

6.3   *Summary*

This chapter discusses the third major characteristic of an object-relational DBMS: support of data and function inheritance. The features required for this support are as follows.

Feature 1: Both data and function inheritance must be supported.

In general, data inheritance by itself is not very useful. The real power comes from inheritance of functions.

Feature 2: Overloading must be supported.

It is highly desirable to be able to specialize the definition of a function to subtypes. This requires the possibility of multiple implementations of functions with the same name.

Feature 3: Types and tables must be separate concepts.

This chapter assumes a type hierarchy with separately defined containers (tables) to hold instances. In this case, you can have multiple tables of a specific type, for example, eastern_emp and western_emp. Each automatically has the inheritance properties described in this chapter. In contrast, some systems make the table hierarchy the same thing as the type hierarchy. Here, there can only be one table for a specific type, and considerable flexibility is forfeited.

Feature 4: Multiple inheritance must be supported.

In many applications, such as the example illustrated in this chapter, a given type must inherit from two different supertypes. Only support for multiple inheritance allows this to happen.

CHAPTER 7   *Characteristic 4: Rules*

The last required feature in a good object-relational DBMS is a powerful general-purpose rules system. Rules are exceptionally valuable in most DBMS applications because they protect the integrity of data in a database. (You have already encountered one example of a business rule, referential integrity, which is discussed on page 57.) Although relational systems provide some support for rules through the use of triggers, object-relational DBMSs demand a much more flexible system.

The paradigm for rules in DBMSs is a production system, popularized in the 1980s by the artificial intelligence community. The general form of a rule is

on event

do action

Thus, rule semantics require a system to watch for an occurrence of the desired event and then execute the appropriate action. Rule systems must include the capability of executing the action just before or just after the event is processed, and typically default to just after execution. This chapter discusses the following four variations of the basic paradigm:

- Update-update rules
- Query-update rules

- Update-query rules
- Query-query rules

7.1   *Update-Update Rules*

The first kind of rule is one where the event is an update and the action is another update. Consider the following rule, which watches for an update to Mike's salary and then propagates the change on to Jane:

```
create rule new_update_update as
on update to emp.salary where current.name = 'Mike'
do update emp
            set salary = new.salary
            where name = 'Jane';
```

Suppose that Mike's salary is $52,000 and his co-worker Jane's salary is $45,000. When Mike's salary is updated, Jane's is also, according to the update-update rule. For example, the following update

```
update emp
set salary = '52500'
where name = 'Mike';
```

will, as a side effect, adjust Jane's salary to $52,500.

This update-update rule watches for the event that updates Mike's salary. When this event occurs, an action is automatically performed, namely to propagate the salary adjustment on to the employee Jane. The action is any legal SQL statement, augmented by the keyword new. New.salary refers to the field in the updated record at the time the event occurs, and it is used to provide a data value to the action.

Of course, at the same time, Mike's old salary can also be propagated on to Emma's salary:

```
create rule old_update_update as
on update to emp.salary where current.name = 'Mike'
do update emp
            set salary = current.salary
            where name = 'Emma';
```

When Mike receives a salary adjustment, co-worker Emma's salary is set to Mike's old salary, while Jane receives Mike's new salary. Thus, as a result of side effects from the following update,

```
update emp
set salary = '56000'
where name = 'Mike';
```

Emma's salary will be set to $52,500 and Jane's to $56,000.

It is possible to have very general rules, for example,

```
create rule bonus_40_update as
on update to emp.salary where current.startdate < '1980-01-01'
do update emp
                set salary = new.salary + (500)
                where current.name = emp.name;
```

In this example, whenever an employee who started before 1980 receives a salary adjustment, the employee also gets a $500 raise.

In other database systems update-update rules are often called "triggers." They are very useful in supporting data integrity in a database. When an event occurs that causes an integrity violation, then the corresponding corrective action can be performed as the action part of an update-update rule. In fact, with the Illustra server, referential integrity is supported by converting each referential integrity declaration into an update-update rule that is then enforced by the Illustra engine.

7.2   *Query-Update Rules*

The second kind of rule is a query-update rule. With this rule the event is a query and the action that is taken is an update. An example of this second kind of rule is

```
create rule query_update as
on select to emp.salary where current.name = 'Mike'
do insert into audit values
                (current.salary, user, current_timestamp);
```

Here, the rule watches for an event, which in this case is to retrieve Mike's salary. If this event occurs, then an insert is made into an audit table indicating who made the request (user), the value received (salary), and the time of the request (current_timestamp). The audit table uses this information to maintain a complete record of accesses to Mike's salary. Such audit trails are usually very difficult to code in the trigger systems offered by other vendors because they do not support query-update rules.

7.3   *Update-Query Rules*

The third kind of rule is an update-query rule. Here, the event is an update and the action is to generate a response to a user. In other contexts, update-query rules are commonly called "alerters." The Illustra server supports a very powerful alerting system that is specified using two statements:

```
create alerter my_alert
        (mechanism = 'callback');

create rule update_query as
        on update to emp.salary where current.name = 'Mike'
        do alert my_alert;
```

The second statement defines an update-query rule that watches for an update to Mike's salary and takes an action to notify an alerter, in this case my_alert. This alerter is created in the first statement, which also indicates how clients will receive notification of this alert (by callback).

It is also possible to specify that clients will poll the server to receive notification of alerts that have occurred since the last time they polled. A client indicates interest in an alert by using the **listen** statement:

listen [my_alert]

Any number of clients can listen for the same alert and a client can listen for multiple alerts. A client listening on one or more alerts then goes about the business of doing queries and running transactions.

Some subset of the alerts have a poll mechanism rather than a callback mechanism. For those alerts, the client must periodically poll the server to receive notification of the alerts that have fired since the last time the client polled. The syntax is

poll

The remaining alerters are specified as "callback." In this case, the Illustra server signals the application asynchronously that the event has occurred.

Callback is especially relevant for applications that have the sole task of listening for alerters that correspond to (say) abnormal events and then take appropriate corrective action. Industrial plant monitoring systems are often of this form. In such systems, the client wishes to listen for a collection of alerters and idles pending notification of the first one.

7.4 *Query-Query Rules*

The fourth kind of rule is a query-query rule. In this situation, the event is a retrieval and the action to be taken is also a retrieval. In the example on page 88 Mike's salary was propagated on to Jane using an update-update rule. The exact rule was

```
create rule update_update as
on update to emp.salary where current.name = 'Mike'
do update emp
            set salary = new.salary
            where name = 'Jane';
```

Using this scheme an update-update rule enforced that two employees had identical salaries. However, there is another way to accomplish the same goal with a query-query rule:

```
create rule query_query as
on select to emp.salary where current.name = 'Jane'
do instead
        select salary
        from emp
        where name = 'Mike';
```

This rule watches for an event that retrieves Jane's salary. When this event occurs, an action is performed. In this example, the action is to retrieve Mike's salary. In addition, the keyword **instead** indicates that the action is to be performed instead of the event that caused the rule to fire. As a result, the following query returns Mike's salary rather than Jane's:

```
select salary
from emp
where name = 'Jane';
```

Thus, Jane's salary is never actually selected and is a *virtual* data element. Mike's salary is physically stored and returned whenever either Jane or Mike's salary is requested. This is another way to ensure that Jane and Mike make the same salary, namely to store only one salary and then return it as a result of two different queries. Of course, it is possible to update Jane's salary, for example,

```
update emp
set salary = 100000
where name = 'Jane';
```

This statement will store the value 100,000 in Jane's salary attribute. However, the query-query rule will take precedence and always return Mike's salary instead.

Another use of query-query rules is to specify more elaborate protection systems than are possible with normal SQL systems. Specifically, traditional SQL systems have a grant/revoke security system that authorizes users to access tables and views, but only gives them data if they are authorized. Unfortunately, a persistent user can often glean information from such a security system. Suppose, for example, a particular user, Mark, is authorized to read employee salaries below $10,000. This can be accomplished by giving Mark access to the following view:

```
create view mark_emp as
select name, salary
from emp
where salary < 10000;
```

Suppose Mark then runs the query:

```
select name, salary
from mark_emp
where name = 'Emma';
```

A null return means that Emma earns more than $10,000, and Mark has received some privileged information about Emma. As you can see, it is possible for SQL security systems to leak some information.

A more dramatic protection scheme now follows. Suppose the following query-query rule is defined:

```
create rule query_query as
on select to emp.salary where current.salary >= 10000
        do instead
        return rand_salary();
```

In this case, if Mark asks for Emma's salary, he will receive a random number from which he can derive no useful information. Other users who are properly authorized will receive the correct answer; thus, a query-query rule system can be made to *lie* to unauthorized users instead of giving them nothing.

You can put any collection of SQL statements into the action part of a rule and create composite rules that combine aspects of the four basic kinds of rules—update-update, update-query, query-update, and query-query. For example, the following rule is perfectly legal:

```
create rule query_update as
        on select to emp.salary where current.name = 'Jane'
        do instead begin
                insert into audit values
                        (current.salary, user, current_time)
                select unique salary from emp where name = 'Mike'
        end;
```

As a result of a query to Jane's salary, the object-relational engine is asked to take two actions: one is an update to log the access in an audit trail and the second is a query to return to Mike's salary as the answer.

A rule system such as the one above is a very powerful vehicle for supporting sophisticated DBMS applications. Not only can you trigger extra actions as a result of user updates, but you can also construct tailored audit trails, sophisticated alerting systems, virtual data elements, and elaborate protection. No doubt, as more experience is gained with rule systems, additional uses for these constructs will emerge.

Unfortunately, there is a dark side to rules; as you will see in the following section, they pose certain semantic difficulties.

7.5 *Semantics: The Dark Side of Rules*

It is possible to create some fairly weird (and undesirable) effects with certain kinds of rules. This section describes four potential semantic traps to be wary of:

- Multiple rules firing the same event sometimes cause unpredicted results.
- Chain rules can initiate infinite loops.
- Terminating a transaction also aborts the action part of a rule.
- Timing of rule activation can make a difference in the ultimate state of the database.

Multiple Rules Fired by the Same Event

The first thing to notice is that you can define an arbitrary number of rules. As a result, multiple rules can be fired as a result of the same event. Consider, for example, the following two rules:

```
create rule strange_1 as
        on update to emp.salary where current.name = 'Mike'
        do update emp
                set salary = new.salary
                where name = 'Jane';
create rule strange_2 as
        on update to emp.salary where current.name = 'Mike'
        do update emp
                set salary = 2 * new.salary
                where name = 'Jane';
```

In this case, two rules are fired as a result of an update to Mike's salary. The first rule sets Jane's salary to Mike's new salary and the second sets it to twice that amount. Notice that a single data element (Jane's salary) is set to two different values by the two rules. It is important to note that rules that are fired by the same event are executed in a system-determined order. There is no way for a user to control the order of execution of the action parts of multiple rules. As a result, Jane's ultimate salary will depend on the execution order of the above rules.

If Mike's salary is set to $57,000 by the following SQL command,

```
update emp
set salary = 57000
where name = 'Mike';
```

then we cannot know whether Jane's salary will be $57,000 or $114,000.

This situation is analogous to the case of two users each running a transaction that adjusts Jane's salary at nearly the same time. In this case, Jane's ultimate salary will depend on which transaction committed first, something that is not controllable by the users.

To summarize, avoid constructing multiple rules with conflicting actions that can be fired by the same event. The result of such rules is not predictable.

Chain Rules Can Cause Infinite Loops

Chains of rules can be constructed where the action part of one rule makes the event of the next rule true. Consider the following two rules:

```
create rule chain_1  as
        on update to emp.salary where current.name = 'Mike'
        do update emp
                set salary = new.salary
                where name = 'Jane';
```

```
create rule chain_2 as
        on update to emp.salary where current.name = 'Jane'
        do update emp
                set salary = new.salary
                where name = 'Sam';
```

Suppose we update Mike's salary:

```
update emp
set salary = 58000
where name = 'Mike';
```

This update to Mike's salary fires "chain_1," which will propagate the new salary on to Jane's salary, which will cause "chain_2" to fire, further propagating the update on to Sam.

Unfortunately, it is also possible to construct chains of rules that are ill-formed. Consider the following two rules:

```
create rule bad_1
        on update to emp.salary where current.name = 'Mike'
        do update emp
                set salary = 2 * new.salary
                where name = 'Jane';
```

```
create rule bad_2
        on update to emp.salary where current.name = 'Jane'
        do update emp
                set salary = 2 * new.salary
                where name = 'Mike';
```

An update to either Jane or Mike's salary circularly fires bad_1 and bad_2, leading a system into an infinite loop. A good object-relational DBMS must notice this condition and do something reasonable; for example, execute the loop exactly once. Clearly, you should avoid constructing rules such as these.

Aborting the Action Part of a Rule Terminates the Whole Transaction

Another issue that concerns the semantics of rules deals with the transaction in which the action part of a rule executes. Normally, the action is executed in the same transaction that caused the rule to fire. Note that the action part of the rule will abort if you abort your transaction. In most cases this sequence is desirable. For example, return to the update-update rule dealing with Mike and Jane:

```
create rule update_update as
        on update to emp.salary where current.name = 'Mike'
        do update emp
               set salary = new.salary
               where name = 'Jane';
```

If you update Mike's salary and then abort the transaction, also abort the triggered update to Jane's salary.

However, there are situations where this is not the desired effect. Return to the query-update rule from the previous section:

```
create rule query_update as
        on select to emp.salary where current.name = 'Mike'
        do insert into audit values
               (current.salary, user, current_time);
```

In this case, if you retrieve Mike's salary and then abort the transaction, the insert to the audit trail is aborted. Obviously, the purpose of the audit trail is to log salary accesses, and aborting a read transaction can circumvent the intent of the rule.

To do the right thing, the action part of the rule must run in a separate transaction from the user's statement. This other transaction always commits, regardless of the outcome of the user's transaction. It is desirable to be able to specify whether the action will run as a separate transaction or as part of the user's transaction. Currently, there are no known mainstream commercial DBMS rule systems with this flexibility.

Knowing When Rules Fire Is Important

A last issue is the time at which the action runs. In most current systems, rules are fired either just before or just after the event is processed. This corresponds to *immediate* execution of rules. In certain applications, you would like rules to fire only when the transaction that activates them actually commits. Currently, such *deferred* execution is not supported in any commercial DBMS that I am aware of.

Both kinds of behavior are desirable. To illustrate the requirement for deferred execution, consider the following rule:

```
on delete emp
then delete dept
where manager = current.name;
```

This rule indicates that when an employee is deleted, the department that he manages must also be deleted. Now consider the following transaction:

```
begin
delete emp
where name = 'John';
update dept
set manager = 'Joe'
where manager = 'John';
end
```

This transaction deletes John and then makes Joe the manager of John's department. If the rule fires at the time of the first update, then John's department is removed. However, at the end of the transaction, there is no department that John manages because the second statement made Joe the manager of any such department; thus, deferred execution of the rule has no effect. In this case, deferred execution is probably what you want to use.

Note that the time the rule is activated can make a difference in the ultimate state of the database at the end of the transaction. Some rules must be run immediately, for example, query-query rules; some can be run either immediately or at the end of the transaction. Ideally, you should be able to specify the timing you want.

7.6   *Summary*

In order for a system to be fully object-relational, it must support a rule system with the following features.

Feature 1: A rule system must support events and actions that are both retrieves and updates.

A system that supports only triggers gives users only a subset of needed capabilities.

Feature 2: The rule system must be integrated with other object-relational capabilities.

For example, the event and action part of a rule must be allowed to be any SQL statement. User-defined functions must be allowed to appear in a rule. In addition, if the object-relational system supports inheritance, then it is crucial that rules be inherited.

Chapter 6 describes an inheritance hierarchy dealing with persons, employees, students, and student employees. In this chapter, numerous rules dealt with the emp table. Because student_emp inherits its behavior from emp, then rules on emp will be inherited by student_emp. Clearly, a rule system requires automatic rule inheritance; you should not have to enter the same rule multiple times, once for each table in a table hierarchy.

Feature 3: A rule system supports {immediate, deferred} and {same transaction, different transaction} execution semantics.

All options are needed to generate the desired semantics for assorted important cases.

Feature 4: The rule system must not loop.

Obviously, the rule system cannot go into an infinite loop. An object-relational engine must have some strategy to recover gracefully from the execution of a circular rule set.

Notice clearly that determining whether a rule set is circular is very difficult. Consider the following slight modification of the rules on page 94:

```
create rule bad.3
     on update to emp.salary where current.name = 'Mike'
do update emp
     set salary = 2 * new.salary
where name = 'Jane';

create rule bad.4
     on update to emp.salary where current.name = 'Jane'
     and current.salary <600000
     do update emp
         set salary = 2 * new.salary
         where name = 'Mike';
```

Whenever Mike or Jane receives a salary adjustment, the two rules will circularly fire. However, the looping behavior ends when Jane's salary is adjusted above $600,000. Therefore, these two rules terminate while the ones on page 94 do not. It is very tough to tell the difference.

CHAPTER 8   *Object-Relational Parsing*

This chapter provides a high-level look at an object-relational parser's design. A parser is responsible for processing the input textual representation into an internal form that is validated and that is a legal SQL statement for existing DBMS objects. In a relational environment the SQL dialect accepted is the same for each installation. However, in an object-relational world, the types, functions, and operators vary from installation to installation.

To discover what SQL is legal on the current machine, an object-relational parser must be completely table-driven from a large database of table, type, and function information. This information is stored in the system catalogs, which are updated as you declare additional tables, types, or functions. Thus, an object-relational parser differs greatly from traditional relational parsers, which are static and hard-coded with (and limited to) the SQL-92 data types and operations on those types.

8.1   *How an Object-Relational Parser Works*

Consider the following table:

```
create table emp of type employee_t(
                              name        varchar(30),
                              salary      int,
                              startdate   date,
                              location    point,
                              picture     image);
```

Here, name, salary, and startdate have the obvious interpretation, while location is a (latitude, longitude) pair corresponding to the employee's home address and picture is an image of the employee.

The following query selects from the emp table:

```
select name
from emp
where salary > 5000
and vesting(startdate) > 0.6
and contained(location, circle ('0,0', 1))
and beard(picture) = 'gray';
```

This query finds all employees whose salary is above $5,000, who are more than 60% vested, whose residence is within a specific circle, and who have a gray beard. The first clause is a comparison of an integer against a constant and is defined in SQL-92. The second clause utilizes a user-defined function on a standard data type. In contrast, the third clause contains a pair of user-defined functions on a non-standard data type. The fourth clause contains a user-defined pattern recognition function, *beard*, that looks at an image and determines whether the person in the image has a beard.

This query presents a challenge to the parser, which must correctly parse a command with user-defined types and functions. To translate SQL queries, the parser uses the following system catalog tables:

- **Tables:** Contains a row for every table in the database, giving the name of the table, the number of columns, and so forth.

- **Columns:** Contains a row for every column of every table in the database, giving the name of the column, its data type, and other information.

- **Types:** Contains a row for every data type known to the current database with the name of the type, its import and export functions, and so forth.

- **Functions:** Contains a row for every function registered in the database, giving the name of the function, the number and types of its arguments, the type of its return, the location of the code for the function, and so forth.

- **Operators:** Contains a row for every operator registered in the database, giving the identity of the function that implements that operator.

There are additional tables in the system catalogs that deal with inheritance, access methods, and rules. These tables are not discussed in this chapter.

The system catalog tables are dynamic; they expand to accommodate new tables, data types, functions, and operators as you define them. When you create a table, the system makes appropriate entries in Tables and Columns. When you create a data type, an entry is made in Types, and similarly, registration of a function causes an insert into Functions. You can think of these tables as metadata, because they contain data about the data in the database. In a relational DBMS, there are metadata only for tables and attributes; types and functions are hard-wired to the SQL-92 definitions.

When an object-relational parser encounters

```
from emp
```

in an SQL command, it looks up emp in Tables to ensure it exists; if emp exists, the parser looks up all the columns of emp in the Columns table. The parser then inserts a descriptor containing this information in a main memory data structure, so that subsequent queries to the same table will not have to pay the overhead of fetching system catalog metadata from disk again.

Much of the query can be parsed based on this information. However, the Functions table must be interrogated for each function noted in the query to ascertain that such a function exists in the current object-relational DBMS installation. Just as it does with Tables and Columns, an object-relational DBMS installation maintains a memory cache for functions so that subsequent uses of the same function do not have to pay any overhead.

It is possible that your query can contain a function with a type mismatch. For example, suppose there is no function *vesting* that takes the data type date as an argument. Instead, suppose *vesting* was defined on the data type century_20. In this case, a parser could give up and declare the SQL query invalid. However, a better option is to correct the type mismatch if possible. To do so, the Illustra system supports the definition of special functions called *casts*. The following command creates a *cast* function:

```
create cast fix_up
from date
to century_20;
```

This declaration indicates that an instance of the data type date can be converted to a corresponding instance of the data type century_20 by calling the function *fix_up*.

If the parser fails to find a *vesting* function for date, it looks for a *vesting* function on a different data type and a *cast* function to that data type. If it finds one, it automatically casts the argument in your query to the new type and then continues parsing using the *vesting* function that exists for this type. Of course, if there are multiple new types to which the argument can be cast, then an ambiguity exists.

Chapter 6 describes how the Illustra system generates an error when inheritance ambiguity is encountered, rather than making an arbitrary choice. The same choice is made here. If a casting ambiguity exists, an error is generated.

8.2   *Summary*

You can now see why a redesign is required to convert a conventional relational parser to an object-relational one. You must rip out all the hard-coded type, operator, and function information, replace it with a table-driven scheme, and then add parser support for SQL syntax for complex objects and inheritance.

CHAPTER 9   *Traditional Relational Optimizers*

This chapter shows how traditional relational optimizers work. It is a prelude to Chapter 10, which discusses the extensions that must be made to support object-relational optimization.

9.1   *How Relational Optimizers Work*

All relational optimizers work roughly the same way and employ variations on the techniques implemented in *System R* by Pat Selinger et al. (1979). Given the traditional example relational tables:

```
create table emp_R (
                    name          varchar(30),
                    salary        int,
                    startdate     date
                    dept          varchar(20));

create table dept_R (
                    dname         varchar(20),
                    floor         int);
```

and given a query such as the following:

```
select name
from emp_R e, dept_R d
where e.dept = d.dname
and d.floor = 1
and e.startdate < '1980-01-01'
and e.salary > 10000;
```

the optimizer will generate a heuristic subset of all possible ways of performing this query. For each such plan evaluated, the optimizer computes the following cost function in a way to be explained in this chapter:

cost = expected number of records examined +
(fudge-factor * (expected number of pages read))

The cost function estimates total resource usage for the query. In effect, the first term is a surrogate for the expected use of CPU resources by the query. The second term guesses the I/O resources and then multiplies them by a fudge factor, indicating for this installation how important CPU resources are relative to I/O resources. The optimizer computes this cost function for a large collection of possible plans and selects the one for execution that has the lowest expected cost.

For the example query, there are restrictions on both the emp_R and dept_R tables and then a join between them. The optimizer assumes that joins are more expensive than restrictions, and therefore examines plans of the form shown in Figure 9.1.

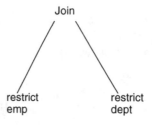

FIGURE 9.1 Join between emp_R and dept_R Tables

This is one of the optimizer's built-in heuristics to minimize the number of plans explored.

9.2 *Performing the Restriction on the Table emp_R*

To perform the restriction on emp_R, there are three possible options to be evaluated:

1. A sequential scan of emp_R
2. An index scan of emp_R using a B-tree index on salary
3. An index scan using a B-tree index on startdate

Sequential Scan of emp_R. Each record of emp_R is evaluated in turn and rejected if the qualification is not true. If there are n-emp records in the table and they occur on N-emp pages, then the cost of this operation is

cost = n-emp + fudge-factor * N-emp

Index Scan of emp_R Using a B-Tree Index on Salary. Most systems employ secondary indexes, where the leaf nodes of a B-tree index contain a collection of records of the form

(indexed-value, pointer-to-a-data-record-with-this-value)

These records are kept in sort order by the B-tree insertion and deletion routines. Figure 9.2 shows a few of the emp_R records and their corresponding leaf B-tree index entries.

In addition, a B-tree has a collection of interior nodes containing records of the form

(value, pointer-to-a-descendent-page)

Typically, the value in any interior record is the highest value found on the descendent page to which the record points. An indexed value can be located by searching the root page for the smallest value that is still greater than the one for which the search is being conducted. Interior pages are searched iteratively until the leaf level is reached, where the value sought can be located. Following the pointer in this leaf record locates the actual data desired. Figure 9.2 shows example entries in the non-leaf portions of the B-tree.

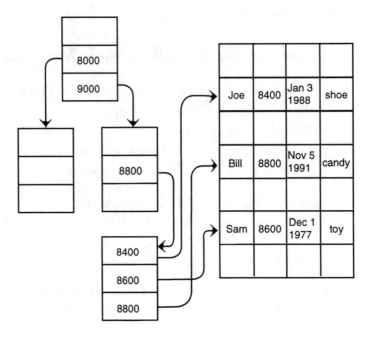

FIGURE 9.2 Example Secondary Index

Range searches can be performed in an analogous way; the above algorithm can be used to find the start of a scan of the leaf-level records in the index. This scan can terminate when an index record is found that is outside the desired range.

Consequently, if a B-tree index for the startdate attribute exists, then an index scan can be performed by using the following clause:

```
salary > 10000
```

For each qualifying index entry, the system must fetch the actual data record for this index record and then evaluate the remaining predicate, namely,

```
startdate < '1980-01-01'
```

To evaluate the expected cost of an index scan, the optimizer must estimate the number of records that satisfy the qualification

```
salary > 10000
```

because this is the number of data records that will be examined. This guess is based on statistical evidence.

Specifically, traditional relational systems allow a database administrator to build a histogram for the salary values in emp_R. For example, the values of salary can be quantized into 10 buckets, 0–2000, 2000–4000, . . . ,18,000–20000, and then the number of emp records that fall within each bucket are computed. This histogram is accurate at the time it is computed and then gradually decreases in accuracy as the emp_R table is updated. Periodically the database administrator must specify that the statistics are to be refreshed.

The optimizer can guess the number of records, K, with salary > 10000 as the sum of the last five buckets in the histogram. If there are no statistics for the salary attribute, then the optimizer must make an arbitrary guess for K. In the Selinger paper (1979), this guess is

$$K = (1/3) * \text{n-emp}.$$

Obviously, such a guess is fairly arbitrary.

The I/O cost of an index scan depends on whether the B-tree index is *clustered* or *unclustered*. If the relational engine attempts to keep the data records in approximately the same order as they appear in the index, that is, the data records are approximately sorted on salary, then the salary index can be called a clustered index. Otherwise, the salary index will be unclustered and the data records are either in random order or approximately ordered on some other attribute. Figure 9.2 showed an unclustered salary index, while Figure 9.3 depicts a clustered version of the same index.

A relational engine ensures clustering by attempting to insert a new data record in storage as close as possible to its correct position in the data set. Therefore, the precision of the clustering is exactly determined by the precision possible at each insert.

If the salary index is unclustered, then the number of I/Os will be approximately equal to the expected number of records examined, a quantity that has already been estimated. The reason for this formula is that each index record contains a pointer to a data record. In an unclustered index, each such record will likely be on a different data page, and one data page must therefore be read per index entry. The cost of an index scan of an unclustered index is

$$\text{cost} = K + \text{fudge-factor} * K$$

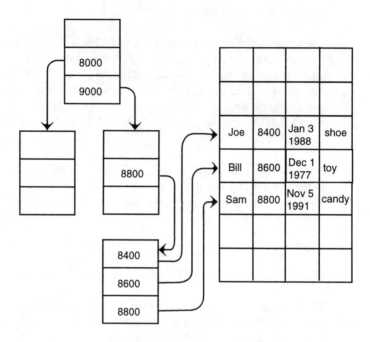

FIGURE 9.3   Example Clustered Secondary Index

In contrast, if the index is clustered, then a different calculation must be made. Specifically the expected number of employee records per data page is

emps-per-page = n-emp / N-emp

Because the optimizer has already estimated K, the number of records that satisfy the qualification

```
salary > 10000
```

then it will estimate that

total-pages = K / emps-per-page

pages must be examined. The reason for this calculation is that employee records are clustered together in the data set in approximately salary order. As the index is scanned, the next record pointer will probably point to the same page as the previous one, and all employees with salaries greater than 10000 will be clustered together on as few pages as possible. The complete cost for an index scan of a clustered index is cost = K + fudge-factor * (K / emps-per-page)

The optimizer now has an estimated cost for an index scan of the emp_R table using the salary index for the two possible organizations of the index.

Index Scan Using a B-Tree Index on Startdate.   The optimizer can use methods similar to those just described to determine whether there is a B-tree index on the startdate attribute and compute the expected cost of an index scan using this index.

Some systems implement an additional way to perform the restriction on emp_R. Specifically, it is possible to build an execution plan that uses both indexes. You can scan the startdate index for pointers to employees that satisfy the qualification

```
startdate < '1980-01-01'
```

and then scan the salary index for pointers to employees that satisfy

```
salary > 10000
```

Then, the two lists of pointers are intersected to find the collection of pointers that satisfies both predicates. As a last step the plan accesses the relevant emp_R records to obtain needed data fields. In certain cases, performing list operations on multiple indexes is an excellent query processing option and is evaluated by some relational engines.

At this point, the optimizer has an expected cost for all possible ways of performing the appropriate restriction on emp_R. In a similar fashion, it can compute the expected cost of the restriction on dept_R, utilizing all possible ways to perform the restriction.

There are two additional steps performed by all optimizers. The first concerns processing predicates containing the negation operation. If the optimizer ever sees a clause of the form

```
where not some-predicate
```

then it can only solve this query using a sequential scan. Thus, when a "not" appears in a predicate, it is impossible to perform an index scan, and the high performance way of running the query is not available.

Therefore, optimizers attempt to remove the not operation from the predicate, by using semantic knowledge of SQL operators. Specifically, the optimizer knows that > is the negation of <=. If the optimizer sees a predicate of the form

```
where not (salary > 10000)
```

it can transform the predicate to

```
where salary <= 10000
```

The operation **not** can be removed from the predicate if the operator inside the predicate is replaced by its negator operator. For all SQL comparison operators {<, <=, =, >, >=, !=}, the optimizer knows the appropriate negator operator and performs the transformation to remove the **not**.

The second modification of a predicate is for bookkeeping convenience. A clause might be written as

```
where   10000   > salary
```

Here, the constant appears on the left-hand side of the operator while the variable is on the right. Alternatively, the clause might have been written with the constant on the right, for example,

```
where salary < 10000
```

Rather than require the execution engine to understand both forms of clauses, SQL optimizers convert the predicate to *canonical form* by transforming each clause in the predicate to have the constant on the right-hand side. This requires optimizers to have knowledge of the commutator operator for each comparison operator. With the knowledge that > is the commutator for <, the optimizer can convert the first representation into the second one. This processing step allows the engine to only deal with predicates in canonical form and simplifies internal bookkeeping.

9.3   *Methods for Processing the Join*

Next, this chapter discusses ways to process the join that remains after the restrictions have been evaluated and two temporary tables, T1 and T2, have been constructed. This join is

```
select T1.name
from T1, T2
where T1.dept = T2.dname;
```

There are three possible techniques that the optimizer must evaluate:

- nested loop join
- merge join
- hash join

All of these techniques require estimates for the number of records and number of pages in both of the tables to be joined. These tables result from restriction operations earlier in the plan. In the example query, the restrictions are

```
select name, dept
from emp_R
where startdate < '1980-01-01'
and salary > 10000;

select dname
from dept_R
where floor = 1;
```

At optimization time these tables do not exist, so the optimizer must guess their resulting size.

In the case of dept_R, the optimizer has previously guessed the selectivity of the clause

```
floor = 1
```

The optimizer can simply multiply this number by n-dept to estimate the number of records in one argument to the join. Similarly, it can multiply this estimate by the width of the dname field to estimate the number of pages in the argument.

However, the corresponding estimates for the restriction on emp_R are more problematic. Estimates for the selectivity of each of the two clauses have been previously computed. Most optimizers simply multiply them together to arrive at a combined selectivity. Of course, this makes the assumption that the clauses are statistically independent, an assumption rarely justified in practice. This independence assumption introduces errors in the size estimates for temporary arguments, which in turn propagate through the rest of the query plan.

The Nested Loop Join Technique. The first technique, nested loops, can be applied by choosing either T1 or T2 as the "outer" table, and then iterating over this table. If T1 is chosen, then each record in T1 is iteratively retrieved, yielding a value for T1.name and T1.dept. These values are substituted into the query, producing

```
select value-1
from T2
where value-2 = T2.dname
```

If there are n-T1 records in T1 occupying N-T1 pages, then the cost of this join strategy is

> n-T1 + fudge-factor * N-T1
>
> +
>
> n-T1 (expected cost of the resulting query on T2)

The nested loops technique constructs a collection of queries on the table T2, which the optimizer then guesses the cost of, using the techniques described earlier. As a result, there are two computations for iterative substitution, namely, 1) choose T1 as the outer table and 2) choose T2 as the outer table.

The Merge-Join Method. The second alternative is to perform merge-join. Here, both T1 and T2 are sorted on the join field, if they are not already in sort order. After one or two sorts, the two tables are correctly ordered on the same attribute and the two tables can be merged by stepping through both tables in an orderly fashion to produce the joined result. The cost of merge-join is

> cost (sort T1) + cost (sort T2) + cost (merge)

The cost of a sort is determined by the algorithm employed. However, most vendors choose a polyphase sort algorithm. Using this algorithm, the CPU cost of the sort is

> constant-1 * n * log n

where n is the number of records being sorted. In addition, the number of pages examined is also

> constant-2 * N * log N

where N is the number of pages being sorted. For details on the composition of the two constants as well as the base of the logarithm in the calculation, consult a text on sorting, such as Knuth (1973).

The cost of the merge operation is simply

> n-T1 + n-T2 + fudge-factor * (N-t1 + N-T2)

Adding the three costs together gives the ultimate cost of merge-join as a join strategy.

The Hash-Join Algorithm. The last alternative is the hash-join algorithm. Here, one table is selected and hashed on the join field into a collection of H hash buckets. If there is enough main memory to hold all H buckets, then the algorithm proceeds by sequentially reading the second table for each record hashing on the join field to produce a hash bucket. Then the appropriate hash bucket is searched to see whether a matching record or records is found. In this case, the CPU cost of a hash-join is

n-T1 + n-T2 * (number of records in a hash bucket)

This latter quantity is simply

n-T1 / H

Similarly, the I/O cost is merely the total sizes of both of the tables:

N-T1 + N-T2

Hash-join has I/O that is linear in the number of pages but a CPU cost that is proportional to

(N-T1 * N-T2)/ H

It may be more or less attractive than merge-join depending on the value assigned to the fudge-factor. Lastly, if there is not enough space in main memory to hold all of one table, then the above algorithm must be modified to utilize less memory. For the details of these modifications, consult a paper on the subject such as Dewitt et al. (1990).

Notice that both hash-join and merge-join are only possible if the join is an equality join, such as in our example. If the join clause does not use equality, then only a nested loop join is possible.

Furthermore, if there are multiple join clauses that connect two tables, then the optimizer must evaluate each one according to the above computations. The other join predicates then become restrictions on the table that is produced as a result of the join.

If you specify a three-way join, then the optimizer must evaluate all possible ways of performing the first join. The result of the first join must then be joined with the remaining table. To compute the cost of this final operation, the optimizer must generate an estimate for the size of the result of the first join. The optimizer has available the expected sizes of the two tables that are to be joined together; however, it must construct an estimate for the size of the answer. Obviously, the number of records in a join can vary from

none—that is, no records from one table join with any records in the other one

to

n-T1 * n-T2—that is, every record in the first table joins to every record in the second table.

Of course, the latter outcome only happens in rare circumstances. For example, if only one value for the join field is present in each table and they match, then the resulting join will have n-T1 * n-T2 records.

To construct an estimate for the size of the join, the optimizer requires an estimate for the join selectivity, S (T1, T2). With this estimate, it can compute the expected size of the answer as

S(T1, T2) * n-T1 * n-T2

The above calculation is notoriously imprecise. Generally, n-T1 and n-T2 are the expected size tables that resulted from earlier computations in the query plan, so you would expect them to be rather imprecise. In addition, most optimizers utilize crude measures for S(T1, T2). For example, if both of the join fields are unique keys in their tables, that is, every value is assuredly different, then S(T1, T2) is estimated to be

min (n-T1, n-T2) / (n-T1 * n-T2)

Here, the optimizer is guessing that the size of the join is the same as the smaller of the two tables. Clearly if both join fields are keys, it can be no larger than this number; however, it can, in reality, be much smaller. As you can see, join selectivities are not an exact science.

When a four- or more way join is computed, the optimizer has additional choices to make. It can restrict its search to so-called *left-only* trees. These are query plans of the form shown in Figure 9.4. In this case, the query plan looks like a tree that goes from lower left to upper right. In addition, only the left-hand side of the join is allowed to be something that results from a previous join, and hence the name *left-only tree*.

Alternatively, the optimizer can also evaluate so-called *bushy* trees, query plans that have the form shown in Figure 9.5.

Some optimizers evaluate only left-only trees as a heuristic simplification to cut down on the size of the optimizer search space. Others evaluate all possible plans.

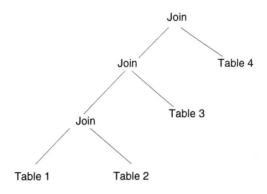

FIGURE 9.4   A Left-Only Tree

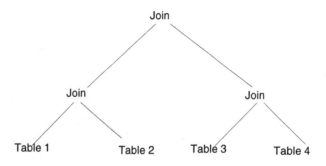

FIGURE 9.5   A Bushy Tree

Optimizers differ widely in the quality of plans that they produce. Generally speaking, most vendors' version 1.0 optimizers are fairly dumb. After a number of release cycles and an infusion of significant development resources, an optimizer becomes smarter. Also, some vendors care more about the quality of their optimizer than others. Unfortunately, the only way to determine who these vendors are is to test each company's optimizer with the kinds of queries that you expect to run.

CHAPTER 10

Object-Relational Optimizers

This chapter examines 15 specific extensions that must be made to a traditional relational optimizer so that it will work well in an object-relational environment. This chapter also offers several test queries to help you ascertain if a particular vendor's optimizer has the necessary object-relational extensions.

The 15 necessary extensions are

14. Optimization of scans of inheritance hierarchies (page 133)

15. Optimization of joins over inheritance hierarchies (page 135)

The examples in this chapter use the emp table from Chapter 8:

```
create type employee_t (
                    name            varchar(30),
                    salary          int,
                    startdate       date,
                    location        point,
                    picture         image);


create table emp of type employee_t;
```

The examples also use a B-tree index defined on the salary attribute as follows:

```
create index salary_index
on emp using B-tree (salary)
```

The relational DBMS vendors' track record for providing straight answers on the quality of their optimizers is poor. For many years one major relational vendor processed join queries in the order that the user constructed the clauses in the predicate. This meant that the order in which the user submitted the joins in the predicate determined the order in which the system processed the joins. This required each user of the system to "hand optimize" each query by putting the predicates in the correct order. Another major relational vendor has not implemented merge-join or hash-join but relies exclusively on nested-loop joins. Therefore, this chapter provides some test queries that you can run to determine whether a particular optimizer does indeed build in each of the necessary extensions.

10.1   *Extension 1: Operator and Function Notation*

Consider a query such as

```
select name
from emp
where salary > 10000;
```

Clearly, the optimizer can utilize either a sequential scan or an indexed scan using salary_index to solve this query. However, in an object-relational DBMS, you can code the salary query in operator notation as above, or you can use the following function notation:

```
select name
from emp
where GreaterThan (salary, 10000);
```

Because these two queries are syntactically different forms of the same query, you should be able to use the notation that you are most comfortable with. Therefore, the optimizer should be able to deal with either notation.

Test for Extension 1. The two representations for the above query are both allowed, and they should generate the same query plan and run at exactly the same speed.

10.2 *Extensions 2 and 3: B-Trees and User-Defined Comparison Operators*

This section discusses the importance of generic B-tree support as well as user-defined comparison operators in an object-relational DBMS. Consider the following query:

```
select name
from emp
where location N_equator_equals point('500, 0')
```

Here, you are requesting the employees who live at the same distance from the equator as the point (500, 0), that is, those employees who live exactly 500 miles north of the equator. The user-defined operator, N_equator_equals, expresses this request.

Obviously, the optimizer can utilize a sequential scan of emp to solve this query. However, a B-tree index scan is generally faster for this query. After all, employees can be sorted on distance north of the equator and then a B-tree can be built on "northness." With such a B-tree, the above predicate can be used to perform an indexed scan, and a more efficient query plan is likely to result.

In order for this query to be able to use an index scan, the following two extensions to an object-relational system are necessary:

- B-tree code must be made generic.
- User-defined comparison operators are required.

In current relational systems, the B-tree code hard-wires numeric date and character string data types. You can build a B-tree only on these specific types. In an object-relational DBMS, the B-tree system must be generic; it must be possible to build a B-tree on any data type, and not just on alphanumeric types. For example, it must be possible to build a B-tree on instances of the point data type.

Moreover, when presented with an equality search such as the one above, the current relational B-tree search logic begins at the root page of the B-tree and searches for the (value, pointer) pair that has the smallest value greater than or equal to the constant in your query. When this (value, pointer) is identified, the B-tree logic retrieves the page identified by the pointer and repeats the procedure. The process concludes when the leaf level is reached and specific pointers to data records are identified. To perform this search, the logic in current B-trees has a hard-wired notion of the definition of "greater than or equal" for each of the alphanumeric types supported.

To solve the above query using an index scan, it must be possible to build a B-tree with user-defined operators instead of the standard alphanumeric comparison operators. A B-tree can support index scans for the operators $\{<, <=, =, >, >=\}$. For user-defined types, such as point, a human must be able to specify the definition of these operators. For example, the following set of comparison operators could be used for the point data type:

- N_equator_greater_than
- N_equator_greater_than_equals
- N_equator_equals
- N_equator_less_than
- N_equator_less_than_equals

There are numerous possible collections of comparison operators for new data types. For example, you can utilize the following possibilities for the point data type:

- Northness, as described in the above example
- Westness, which involves the same general computation as the above example
- Distance away from a specific point, say company headquarters

It is possible to build a B-tree to support any one of these classes of operators. For example, the syntax to construct the appropriate B-tree index in the Illustra system is

```
create index age-index
on emp using B-tree (location, northness-class);
```

Here northness-class defines the collection of five comparison operators mentioned above and instructs the B-tree index to be built using them. All insertions to the B-tree are done using the comparison operator "N_equator_greater_than_equals." The optimizer understands that any query containing one of these five operators is a candidate for an index scan solution.

With generic B-trees and user-defined operator classes, it is possible to build a B-tree index that supports index scans on a wide variety of user-defined data types and operators.

Tests for Extensions 2 and 3. The test for extension 2 is simple; it must be possible to build B-tree indexes on user-defined types with user-defined operators. To test for user-defined comparison operator support, run a query such as the one requesting employees 500 miles north of the equator. Can the query use an index scan with a response time of a second or two for a large employee collection?

10.3 *Extension 4: User-Defined Selectivity Functions*

In a relational DBMS selectivity functions are hard-coded into the optimizer, as discussed in Chapter 9. Clearly, when a new data type and appropriate comparison operators are defined, the optimizer has no possible knowledge of the selectivity of these operators for the new data type. This means there must be a way for you to specify how the optimizer computes selectivities.

In the Illustra system, a B-tree index uses a specific operator class, such as the northness operators discussed above. Each operator in this class is associated with a specific binary function when the operator is created. For example, the following command binds N_equator_equals to the function *Northness_equal*:

```
create binary operator
binding N_equator_equals
to Northness_equal;
```

When you define a new function to the DBMS, you can optionally define a second function associated with it, called a *selectivity* function. This feature enables you to tell the optimizer how to compute the selectivities it must have to properly evaluate plans. The following definition of *Northness_equal* illustrates this construct:

```
create function Northness_equal (point, point)
returns Boolean
with selfunc = selectivity_comp
external name '/usr/Northness_equal'
language C;
```

When the optimizer sees a query such as

```
select name
from emp
where location N_equator_equals point ('500, 0');
```

it will call the function *selectivity_comp* to return a floating-point number between 0 and 1. Then it will multiply this returned value by the size of the emp table to generate an estimate for the number of index records that will be evaluated. The *selectivity_comp* function may construct its value based on statistics, or through some other technique.

Test for Extension 4. It must be possible to specify user-defined selectivity functions to an object-relational DBMS optimizer.

10.4   *Extension 5: User-Defined Negators*

The following example query helps to illustrate user-defined negators:

```
select name
from emp
where not (location N_equator_greater_than point ('500, 0'));
```

Ideally, the optimizer can transform this query to

```
select name
from emp
where location N_equator_less_equal point ('500, 0');
```

The second expression can be evaluated for use of an index scan, while the first cannot. More formally stated, the following transformation occurs:

not (attribute operator value)   ==>   attribute operator-2 value

To make this transformation, the optimizer must be told the negator (operator-2 in the above example) for each user-defined operator.

In the Illustra system, when the function *Northness_greater_than* is constructed, the function creator can optionally specify the negator for the function. For example,

```
create function Northness_greater_than (point, point)
returns Boolean
with negator = Northness_less_equal
external name '/usr/Northness_greater_than'
language C;
```

The following test determines whether a given system supports the optimization of **not.**

Test for Extension 5: Can the two versions of the "less than" query discussed above execute at the same performance, and can they both utilize an index scan?

10.5   *Extension 6: User-Defined Commutators*

This section describes user-defined commutators as a necessary extension for an object-relational optimizer. Consider the following query:

```
select name
from emp
where 500 N_equator_greater_than location;
```

Clearly, this can use an index scan and is equal to

```
select name
from emp
where location N_equator_less_equal 500;
```

Obviously, both queries should run at exactly the same performance. In the Illustra system, this is assured by allowing the definer of a function to specify the commutator for the function as follows:

```
create function Northness_greater_than (point, point)
returns Boolean
with commutator = Northness_less_equal
external name '/usr/Northness_greater_than'
language C;
```

Test for Extension 6. Can the above two specifications of the query run at the same speed, and can both utilize an index scan?

10.6   *Extension 7: Access Methods on a Function of the Data*

Consider the following query:

```
select name
from emp
where redness (picture) < 0.1;
```

This query contains a user-defined function that computes how red an employee's picture is and returns a floating-point number between 0 and 1. It would be desirable to support the possibility of building a B-tree index on the result of the function *redness*. If this index is constructed, then an indexed scan can be utilized to perform the above query.

Traditional relational systems support only B-tree indexes on the value of an attribute. However, there are a variety of data types, including images, where it is never relevant to build an index on the actual attribute. For example, a B-tree index on image data keeps the index in sorted order on the bytes in the image. This index is not relevant to any user queries. Thus, the only plausible indexes are on a function of the image data.

In the Illustra system, function indexes are allowed, and are specified as follows:

```
create index picture_index
on emp using B-tree (redness (picture));
```

This command tells the Illustra system to build an index on the *redness* function, which returns a floating-point number. Comparison operators are those that are appropriate for floats. Moreover, whenever a new employee is added, the Illustra system must compute the *redness* function for the employee's picture and then index the answer. Similarly, when an employee is deleted, the *redness* function must again be computed to find the appropriate index record and remove it. In the unlikely event that an image is updated for an employee, the *redness* function for both the old image and the new image must be computed, so that the index can be appropriately modified.

Notice that the *redness* function is being "eagerly" computed, that is, it is evaluated at the time an employee is added to the data base. In contrast, it would also be possible to evaluate the function at the time it was used in a query, that is using "lazy" evaluation. If an Illustra function is indexed, then it is converted from lazy to eager evaluation. As a result, a query using the function receives much better response time, because the computation need not be performed at runtime. Moreover, the result of the function is indexed, possibly allowing the optimizer to construct a better plan for the query. As a result, function indexing is a very valuable optimization technique.

It is possible in some systems to define a collection of triggers that compute redness in the action part and store the result in a new column in the table. Indexing can then be performed on the stored data. The disadvantage of this scheme is the necessity of storing the extra column. In addition, if the index is no longer needed, it can be tedious to remove the added attribute. Indexes on functions are a much more elegant solution.

Test for Extension 7. It must be possible to construct an index on the *redness* function and the optimizer must automatically use the index when appropriate. Your query must be specified the same way whether the index is present or not.

10.7   *Extension 8: Smart Ordering of the Clauses in a Predicate*

Consider the following modification to the previous query:

```
select name
from emp
where redness (picture) < 0.1 and salary > 10000;
```

and assume for the moment that there are no indexes on the emp table. In this case, a sequential scan must be utilized.

A relational DBMS will perform a sequential scan and evaluate the predicate for each retrieved record. However, it will evaluate the clauses in the predicate from left to right. In traditional SQL, this is a reasonable strategy, since all clauses are generally quite simple and do not involve significant CPU time. Unfortunately, this assumption is not true in an object-relational DBMS, as the above query demonstrates. Specifically, the clause

```
salary > 10000
```

requires perhaps 100 CPU instructions to evaluate, while the clause

```
redness (picture) < 0.1
```

requires perhaps $100 * (10^6)$ instructions. The reason for this computational intensity is that *redness* must perform a color analysis of a large image, which requires significant CPU resources.

If a query plan evaluates clauses from left to right, then *redness* will be evaluated for all employees. In contrast, if the clauses are evaluated from right to left, then *redness* will only be evaluated for the employees who are highly compensated, a much smaller set. Careful attention to the computational requirements of individual clauses can make an enormous difference in the running time of the above query. The traditional relational cost model discussed in the previous chapter,

cost = expected number of records examined +

fudge-factor * (expected number of pages read)

is too primitive to capture the computational requirements of individual clauses.

Specifically, the expected number of records examined is too primitive a measure of CPU usage, because it cannot discriminate between different orderings of the clauses in a predicate. In addition, a traditional optimizer assumes that each record is read in its entirety when computing the expected number of pages read. Again, this assumption is not justified when a function is I/O intensive. For example, it is possible that images are stored with a color histogram at a specific location in the representation. If so, the *redness* function need read only the histogram and not the entire image. In effect, the function's I/O requirement will drop from perhaps one megabyte to tens of kilobytes. Obviously, the optimizer must take this fact into consideration when constructing a query plan.

To keep track of the demands of functions that are expensive in CPU and/or I/O resource utilization, the Illustra system's optimizer uses a more elaborate cost function. And some additional information must be provided when a function is defined. This information is

A = percall-cpu: specifies the per-call CPU cost for the function

B = byte-percentage: specifies the expected percentage of the bytes in the argument that the function will read

C = perbyte-cpu: specifies the CPU cost per byte read

The CPU cost of a function invocation is

$$A + C * (B * \text{expected size of argument})$$

Similarly, the I/O cost is

$$B * \text{expected size of argument}$$

When presented with a query, the Illustra optimizer computes the more detailed cost for each permutation of the clauses in a predicate. The test for extension 8 can easily demonstrate whether an optimizer will deal wisely with expensive functions.

Test for Extension 8. Do the following two queries run at the same speed?

```
select name
from emp
where salary > 10000 and redness (picture) < 0.1;

select name
from emp
```

```
where redness (picture) < 0.1 and salary > 10000;
```

10.8   *Extension 9: Optimization of Expensive Functions*

An extension of the optimization of expensive functions is their correct placement in a query plan. Consider the following somewhat artificial query:

```
select e.name, f.name
from emp e, emp f
where e.salary = f.salary
and redness (e.picture) < 0.1
and redness (f.picture) < 0.1
```

This query finds the pairs of employees who earn the same salary and have low redness images. In a traditional optimizer, the restrictions will always be performed first, leading to the structure shown in Figure 10.1 for the query plans that are evaluated.

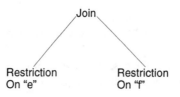

FIGURE 10.1   Restriction, Then Join

This strategy is appropriate when all clauses are inexpensive to compute, as is the case for SQL-92. However, when expensive clauses appear in queries, this strategy may be undesirable. Specifically, it will compute redness for all possible employees. Moreover, unless the optimizer is very smart and caches the result of the first collection of redness computations, it will probably compute redness twice, once to evaluate the restriction on "e" and once for "f." The resulting low redness employees will then be joined on salary.

In contrast, it is probably preferable to perform the join first to find pairs of employees who were born in the same year. Subsequently, you can evaluate each pair for redness. The resulting query plan is shown in Figure 10.2.

Restriction
On Redness

Join of
"e" and "f"

FIGURE 10.2   Join, Then Restriction

If there are few pairs of employees with the same salary, then the latter strategy is preferable. In this case, push the restriction clauses up the query plan through the join, so they are done last. Depending on the complexity of the restriction and the size of the join, this *predicate migration* may or may not be a good idea. A formal presentation of predicate migration appears in Hellerstein and Stonebraker (1993), and a good object-relational DBMS uses this technique when appropriate.

Test for Extension 9. In the case that few employees have the same salary, the above query executes by processing the join first. That is, it executes quickly for a large employee collection.

10.9   *Extension 10: User-Defined Access Methods*

Suppose you submit the following query, which finds employees who live inside a rectangle bounded by the origin and the point (1, 1):

```
select name
from emp
where location contained box ('0,0,1,1');
```

This is a two-dimensional search. Because B-trees are a one-dimensional access method, they are essentially useless in accelerating this query. What is needed is a multidimensional access method such as an R-tree, grid file, quad tree, or K-D-B tree. Similarly, many image applications in the medical and law enforcement field, such as fingerprint recognition and face matching, require finding an image that is close to a given image. In these vertical markets, there are specialized access methods that accelerate such searches. Sophisticated keyword indexing systems for textual documents usually support proximity searching where users request pairs of words in a document within a user-specified distance of each other. Again, specialized access methods are used to accelerate proximity searches.

In other words, an access method is needed that is appropriate to the data type, point. Because there can be a variety of new data types defined to an object-relational DBMS and several may need a customized access method, a good object-relational DBMS must allow type definers to add a new access method.

An access method is merely a collection of functions that are called by the execution engine at appropriate places in the execution of a query plan. These functions perform operations such as

1. Open a scan of an index.
2. Get next record in a scan.
3. Insert record.
4. Delete record.
5. Replace record.
6. Close scan.

In the Illustra DBMS, there are a total of 12 such functions. Because an object-relational DBMS supports user-defined functions and can call them where appropriate, it is straightforward to call user-defined access method functions.

Of course, it is not easy to write an access method. The following tasks must be performed inside access method code:

Locking. Appropriate locks must be set and released on index objects. This requires interacting with the lock management code of the DBMS.

Recovery. Access method code must ensure that the data structures they manage are recovered in the event of a crash. This is accomplished by a combination of logging of index events and/or careful coding. If logging is used, then the access method code must interact with the log manager.

Page Management. Access method code must interact with the DBMS buffer manager when it requires a disk page. To avoid copying pages to a separate location, a good access method will use buffer pool pages in place. This demands careful pinning and unpinning of pages, so that the buffer manager does not inadvertently write an index page out to disk before the access method is through with it.

Another important aspect of a user-defined access method is the mechanism for teaching the optimizer about its characteristics. The basic idea is to generalize the indexing interface using B-trees and hashing as a "template." Specifically, a hash access method supports a single kind of query efficiently:

> attribute = value

In contrast, a B-tree supports five operators:

> attribute < value
>
> attribute <= value
>
> attribute = value
>
> attribute > value
>
> attribute >= value

Earlier in this chapter the concept of an operator class for a B-tree, which described the actual operators used in a specific index, was discussed. In a similar way, an operator class for a hash access method can also be described, consisting of a single operator defining the notion of equality used in a particular index.

To add a new kind of access method, you need merely specify a *template* for the operator class that the access method supports. For example, R-trees have the following template:

> attribute = object
>
> attribute overlaps object
>
> attribute contains object
>
> attribute contained_in object

Then you indicate which instantiation of the template you are using in a specific index. With this information, the optimizer can get to work.

Test for Extension 10. It must be possible for a (sufficiently skilled) user to add a new access method to a good object-relational DBMS.

10.10   *Extension 11: "Flattening" Complex Object Queries*

Consider a function that returns a set of employees such as

```
create function high_salary
returns setof(employee_t)
as external name '/local/lib/high_salary.so'
language C;
```

This function is written in C and identifies (somehow) a set of highly paid employ-ees.

As explained in Chapter 4, you can use such a function anywhere a table is allowed in an SQL query. Therefore, the following query is perfectly legal:

```
select name
from high_salary ()
where startdate > '1990-01-01';
```

In this case, the optimizer has no choice but to materialize the result of the function in the from clause. After that it can evaluate the predicate using a scan of the mate-rialized object and compute the target list for qualifying records. Clearly note that C functions are *opaque*. Since the optimizer cannot look inside them, little optimiza-tion is possible.

In contrast, the optimizer understands the definition of functions that are written in SQL. Therefore, the optimizer can *flatten* queries with SQL functions wherever possible. Consider the following query:

```
select name
from SQL-function ('1980-01-01')
where salary = 18000;
```

where *SQL-function* is defined by:

```
create function SQL-function (date)
returns setof (employee_t) as
        select *
        from emp
        where startdate > $1;
```

This query can be unwound to

```
select name
from (select *
     from emp
     where startdate > '1980-01-01')
where salary = 18000;
```

and then flattened to

```
select name
from emp
where startdate > '1980-01-01'
and salary = 18000;
```

In the case that a B-tree index exists for the salary attribute, the optimizer should solve this resulting query using an indexed scan over salary index. Without flattening this query, a poorer strategy will be selected. Therefore, a good object-relational DBMS flattens queries dealing with complex objects wherever possible. This leads to test 11.

Test for Extension 11: The following query executes in one second or less if a B-tree index for salary exists:

```
select name
from SQL-function ('1980-01-01')
where salary = 18000;
```

10.11   *Extension 12: "In-Line" Sets*

Return to the dept table discussed in Chapter 4, namely,

```
create type dept_t(
                dname          varchar(30),
                floor          int,
                manager        varchar(30),
                phone          phone_t,
                autos          setof(auto_t),
                manager_ref    ref(employee_t),
                colors         setof(varchar(30)),
                workers        setof(ref(employee_t)));
```

```
create table dept of type dept_t;
```

and consider the following query:

```
select autos.name, autos.year
from dept
where floor = 1;
```

In this case, the query is looking for the name and year of all autos owned by a department on the first floor. If there is a B-tree index on floor, then the qualifying departments can be quickly located. After that, the autos for each such department must be found. If autos are stored in the same record with their owning department (an "in-line" representation of sets), then this lookup is very fast. If sets are stored in a separate record and then accessed using a level of indirection, then finding the qualifying autos is much slower.

Obviously, a system that uses in-line storage for sets and then overflows to a separate location only when the set becomes very large will dramatically out-perform a system that blindly stores sets in a separate place. This leads to test 12.

Test for Extension 12. A good object-relational DBMS must store "small" sets using an in-line representation.

10.12   *Extension 13: Indexes on Attributes of Sets*

Return again to the dept table mentioned above and consider the following query:

```
select name
from dept
where autos.year = 1982;
```

This query will identify those departments that possess a 1982 automobile. Although it is certainly possible to perform a sequential scan of dept to solve this query, a good object-relational DBMS allows the user to build a B-tree index on the year attribute for all auto instances in any set in the dept table. In other words, the system should support building an index on an attribute of a set. With such an index, the above query will use an index scan and a sequential scan will be avoided.

Test for Extension 13: A good object-relational DBMS must support building indexes on attributes of sets.

10.13   *Extension 14: Optimization of Scans of Inheritance Hierarchies*

The last two optimizations deal with efficiently processing queries whose scope is an inheritance hierarchy. Extension 14 deals with index and table scans. Consider the following two queries and the person/emp/student/student_emp hierarchy illustrated in Figure 6.2 on page 77:

```
select name
from only (emp)
where salary = 10000;
```

```
select name
from emp
where salary = 10000;
```

The first query requests only employees with the correct salary, while the second requests the table hierarchy be "exploded."

It is clearly reasonable for a system to decompose the second query into two actual queries and then run them separately. In this case, the cost of the second query is about twice the cost of the first one. Alternately, it will be much faster to use one query plan with a scope of two tables. With a "union table" node in the plan tree, the bookkeeping associated with the extra queries can be avoided. Of course, if some of the tables have an index on salary and some don't, then a single plan is inappropriate. This discussion leads to the test for extension 14.

Text for Extension 14: It must be possible to index tables in an inheritance hierarchy so that both of the above queries run in a few seconds. Moreover, the cost of the second query should be less than twice the cost of the first one, assuming each table has the same number of instances.

10.14 *Extension 15: Optimization of Joins over Inheritance Hierarchies*

Return to the person/emp/student/student_emp hierarchy illustrated in Figure 6.2 on page 77 and consider the following join query:

```
select e.name
from emp e, dept d
where e.dept = d.dname and d.floor = 1;
```

This query finds all employees and student employees who work on the first floor. The naive way to process this query is to replace it with two actual queries:

```
select e.name
from only (emp) e, dept d
where e.dept = d.dname and d.floor = 1;
```

```
select s.name
from only (student_emp), dept d
where s.dept = d.dname and d.floor = 1;
```

These two join queries can be subsequently executed on their associated tables. It is possible that the optimizer will perform an indexed scan of dept followed by a nested loop join on the result to emp and student_emp, respectively. Notice that the same index scan of dept is being performed twice. Performing duplicate work is obviously a bad idea. Moreover, as the inheritance hierarchy gets deeper, the amount of repetitions done by the naive strategy increases dramatically.

A better solution is to strategically put a "union table" node into the plan tree below the join as shown in Figure 10.3. With this optimization, the duplication of work noted above is removed. This leads to the test for extension 15.

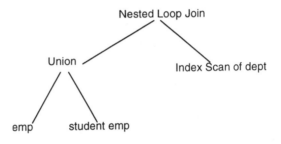

FIGURE 10.3   Using a Union Table

Test for Extension 15. The above example join query over the inheritance hierarchy should run faster than the two table-specific queries, which have the same functionality.

10.15 *Summary*

Fifteen extensions are needed to turn a traditional relational optimizer into a good object-relational optimizer. To make such a conversion, all of the relational DBMS's hard-coded knowledge about fixed data types must replaced with a table-driven system that can support user definition of types, functions, selectivity functions, operator classes, negators, commutators, and access methods. Complex objects and inheritance must also be efficiently treated by the optimizer. I/O or CPU intensive functions must be optimized by extending the cost function evaluated by the optimizer to include more information, and by removing search space reduction tactics, such as always performing restrictions before joins. Just as with parsers, discussed in Chapter 8, the transformation of an optimizer from relational to object-relational requires a major rewrite effort.

CHAPTER 11

Implementation of Rule Systems

This chapter discusses the implementation of rule systems for object-relational systems. It begins with the specific case of triggers. Triggers are update-update rules, one of the four cases discussed in Chapter 7. Triggers are widely implemented by relational DBMSs; the general form is

> on update-condition

> do update-action

Later in the chapter the more general case is discussed where the condition and action can be either retrieves or updates.

11.1 *Support for Triggers*

There are two ways to support triggers. One entails low-level hooks in the executor, and the other involves a procedure called *query modification*. This chapter explains only the simple case where execution of a trigger does not cause other triggers to be activated. Dealing with cascading triggers is more complicated.

Modifying the Executor

Consider the following update-update rule introduced in Chapter 7, which propagates Mike's salary on to Jane:

```
create rule update_update as
on update to emp.salary where current.name = 'Mike'
do update emp
    set salary = new.salary
    where name = 'Jane';
```

When specified to the DBMS, this rule is compiled into an internal form and stored in a table (or tables) in the system catalogs. An identifier for this rule is inserted into the Table table of the system catalogs and is placed in the row that corresponds to the emp table. This makes it easy to ascertain which rules apply to any given table in the database.

When an update occurs, for example,

```
update emp
    set salary = 58000
    where name = 'Mike';
```

the query engine can note that one or more triggers are relevant to the emp table and might be fired during the execution of the command. Therefore, it retrieves the data structure for the appropriate triggers. The optimizer receives the parse tree and develops a query plan for the command as discussed in Chapter 9. In this example, it might be an index scan for a B-tree index on the name attribute of emp. As a last step in plan construction, each of the possibly relevant triggers is grafted onto the plan. The predicate in the update-condition, in this case,

```
where name = 'Mike'
```

is inserted into the query plan, so that two predicates are checked while executing the plan as noted in Figure 11.1. One is the real one from the user's query, while the second is the condition from the possibly relevant trigger. Whenever the real predicate evaluates to true, then the appropriate update is performed, and the old and new instances of the record are readily available in the executor. These are made available to the grafted predicate, which is then evaluated. If it is true, then the action part of the trigger is processed by the executor before continuing with the index scan of the emp table. Thus, triggers are readily supported by grafting possibly relevant triggers onto the query plan for the user's query.

Notice that this implementation supports *immediate* execution of triggers, which was one of the semantics described in Chapter 7. The reason for immediate execution is because the action part of the rule is executed as soon as a relevant record is identified during execution. To support *deferred* execution, substantial additional work must be performed, namely, the above processing must be done to identify triggers that may have to fire at transaction commit time. Rather than executing the action part of each trigger, it is simply saved in a list in the executor. Moreover, the

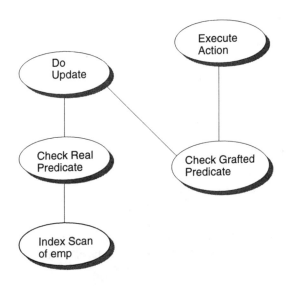

FIGURE 11.1 A Query Plan after Grafting

before value and after value of each updated record must be saved so that the action part of the rule can be executed at commit time, if the condition part of the rule is still valid. Because these values must be saved in the log for crash recovery purposes anyway, it is possible to obtain these values at commit time by reading the log. Alternatively, they can be saved in a form more amenable to commit time processing.

Then, at commit time, the condition part of each trigger in the list must be checked for each before and after image previously identified to ascertain that the condition of the trigger is still true. Because it is possible that a subsequent update in the same transaction made database modifications so that the condition is no longer true, it is necessary to recheck the condition at commit time. If the condition is still true, then the action part of the trigger is executed.

This is a high-level look at deferred execution of triggers. For more extensive treatment of this topic consult Widom and Ceri (1995). There currently are no commercial relational DBMSs that I am aware of that implement deferred execution of triggers at commit time, although several systems allow actions to be deferred until the end of the current SQL command.

Query Modification

The second implementation choice for triggers is a process called *query modification*. To understand this concept, consider the same rule used above:

```
create rule update_update as
on update to emp.salary where current.name = 'Mike'
do update emp
     set salary = new.salary
     where name = 'Jane';
```

as well as the same user command:

```
update emp
     set salary = 58000
     where name = 'Mike';
```

In this case, the same marking is placed in the system catalogs as was done in the first implementation option, so that the parser can recognize the potentially relevant rules for each arriving user query.

For each such rule, query modification is performed to replace the user's statement with a different collection of statements. In the case that the command is an update and the action part of the rule is also an update, query modification is straightforward. Specifically, the user's original statement is run, along with a second command that implements the correct effect of the trigger. In this example, the two commands that are executed are

```
update emp
     set salary = 58000
     where name = 'Mike';
```

```
update emp j
set salary = 58000
where j.name = 'Jane' and
exists (select *
     from emp m
     where m.name = 'Mike');
```

The first statement is simply the unmodified user's statement. The second statement is constructed by substituting the user's statement into the action part of the rule. Intuitively, the second statement gives the correct salary adjustment to Jane, but only if there exists a Mike in the emp table. If Mike does not exist, then the user's command has no effect and the trigger also has no effect. On the other hand, if Mike exists, then his new salary should be propagated to Jane. Thus, the second command performs the correct update to the database.

With either implementation of rules, be aware that the overhead is proportional to the number of potentially relevant rules. If there are R rules on the emp table, then the first implementation will graft R predicates onto the user's query. In the second implementation, a total of R + 1 commands will actually be run. To a first approximation, rules introduce an overhead for a command to a table that is proportional to the number of rules defined for that table. Keep this fact in mind when you use the rule system.

The two implementations have somewhat different performance envelopes. In the example used above, the first implementation offers lower overhead. After all, only one query plan is executed, and the low level grafting should not slow down execution dramatically. In contrast, the second implementation requires two commands to be run.

However, there are cases where the second implementation is faster, as the following example illustrates. Consider the following rule:

```
create rule update_update-2 as
on update to emp.salary where current.name > 'm'
do update emp
     set salary = 10000
     where name = 'Jane';
```

and the command

```
update emp
set salary = 20000
where startdate >=  '1980-01-01'
```

If there are M employees with startdates after 1979 whose last names begin with letters that are in the second half of the alphabet, then the rule will be fired in the first implementation M times and each time the same additional update is performed. Thus, there will be dramatic overhead added to the execution of the user's command. In contrast, the second implementation will perform the following two commands:

```
update emp
set salary = 10000
where startdate >= '1980-01-01';
```

```
update emp
set salary = 20000
where name = 'Jane'
and exists (select name
            from emp
            where name > 'm'
            and startdate >= '1980-01-01');
```

In this case, the second command will ascertain that there exists an employee whose last name begins wih a letter from the second half of the alphabet, and who has an appropriate start date. If so, the update to Jane will be performed exactly once. As a result, the second implementation will be noticeably faster in this case.

Clearly, both implementations will be preferred in different circumstances, and there is no clear performance winner. Most relational DBMSs use some variation of the first implementation. Moreover, some vendors have even implemented special case code for referential integrity, rather than simply turning referential integrity syntax into the appropriate triggers to be implemented by the standard trigger system. The reason for a special case implementation is to achieve higher performance.

11.2   *Extension to More General Rules*

To support a more general rule system, there are extensions that are required to either of the two implementations above. Consider a query-query rule, such as the one from Chapter 7:

```
create rule query_query as
on select to emp.salary where current.name = 'Jane'
do instead
     select salary
     from emp
     where emp.name = 'Mike';
```

In this case, it is fairly straightforward to extend either implementation to behave correctly. The actions that must be taken to support rule execution in this case are local to the scope of the current user's command and grafting or query modification must merely be extended to cover additional cases. However, there are other cases where this locality is not present. For example, consider the following example from Chapter 7:

```
create alerter my_alert
     (mechanism = 'callback');
```

```
create rule update_query as
      on update to emp.salary where current.name = 'Mike'
      do alert  my_alert;
```

and suppose a second user process indicates interest in the alert by

```
listen my_alert;
```

In this case, there are several additional difficulties that must be dealt with. First, the application program interface (API) must be extended with a listen command. Moreover, the structure of the current API must be changed. Specifically, in current systems the application submits a command and then controls the way processing of the command is accomplished through cursor commands. The DBMS is *passive* and expects instructions from the application concerning how to proceed. In contrast, when alerters are present, the DBMS must be *active* and be able to communicate asynchronously to the client application. This requires some reworking of the libraries that support the API.

Lastly, a DBMS that supports alerters must be extended with a communication path between the updating user, who gives Mike a salary adjustment, and the listening user who wants to be notified. This requires the first DBMS task to notify the second one, who can then deliver the alert to the user.

Moving beyond a trigger system to a general-purpose rule system is a fair amount of work. Both deferred execution of rules, as well as retrieve rules, cause this implementation complexity.

CHAPTER 12

Architectural Options for Commercial Vendors

The major players in the object-relational arena are Illustra, Omniscience, and UniSQL. All three are start-up companies that have written object-relational engines from scratch. These systems are designed to solve problems that appear in the upper-right quadrant of the two-by-two matrix introduced in Chapter 1.

Relational vendors, on the other hand, have engines that are carefully optimized for upper-left quadrant problems. As you learned in the last four chapters, major surgery on all parts of the system is required to transplant a DBMS from the upper-left quadrant to the upper-right quadrant.

Basically, to convert from a relational engine to an object-relational one, the following steps are required:

1. Rework the parser to be table-driven.
2. Rework the optimizer to be table-driven and include expensive function optimization and support for inheritance and complex objects.
3. Rework the executor to support secure user-defined functions that are dynamically linked.
4. Rework the access method interface to be open to new implementations.
5. Rework the B-tree code to be generic.
6. Rework storage management to support large data types.

7. Rework the client API so that more general queries can be run and their results returned.

Because the modifications required to a relational engine are so dramatic, amounting to a near complete rewrite, there are several possible architectural options available to the relational vendors. Each option offers different performance characteristics, time to market, and risk. The first four options can be developed solo, while the last two require a partnership with a second vendor who has an object-relational engine.

The four solo strategies are

1. Do nothing.
2. Rewrite the engine from scratch.
3. Iteratively evolve the current engine by adding new functionality.
4. Write a "wrapper."

The strategies that require a partnership with an object-relational vendor are

5. Implement a gateway from an object-relational engine to a relational one.
6. "Glue" the execution engine of an object-relational system onto a relational engine's storage manager.

It's also possible for object-oriented DBMS vendors to build a product that fits in the upper-right quadrant of the matrix. Besides options 1 and 2 listed above, the object-oriented vendor has the following possibilities:

7. Extend an object-oriented DBMS to support object-relational functionality.
8. "Glue" an object-relational engine onto the top of an object-oriented DBMS.

This chapter focuses on the choices available to vendors that currently sell relational or object-oriented DBMSs but wish to move to object-relational technology to "catch the next wave." This chapter discusses all of the listed options and indicates which vendors have selected each of the possibilities. Several vendors have not yet disclosed their object-relational strategy, so the vendor information provided is not complete. Specifically, Informix, Oracle, and Sybase have indicated they are working on object-relational technology but have not yet disclosed their detailed approach. Watch the trade publications for product announcements from these vendors.

12.1 *Strategy 1: Do Nothing*

The first option is always available, that of doing nothing. However, it is a very dangerous strategy for a relational vendor to follow. As noted in Chapter 1, there is an increasing subset of DBMS customers with data processing applications in the upper-left quadrant of the matrix who will add complex data to their environments and thereby move their applications to the upper-right, object-relational quadrant. Certainly, for the foreseeable future there will be many applications that will be forms-based bread-and-butter business data processing applications. However, a significant subset will migrate from the upper-left quadrant to the upper-right, the object-relational side.

Doing nothing will ensure that a relational vendor misses this market shift and loses out on the growing upper-right quadrant market. The "do nothing" strategy only makes sense if a company believes there is no significant market in the upper-right quadrant. It is telling that all relational vendors appear to be working on product enhancements that include support for complex data and that not one is doing nothing.

In contrast to the applications in the upper-left quadrant that are moving quickly to the right, the core of lower-right quadrant applications exhibit no dramatic upward movement. Therefore, because it is less compelling for an object-oriented DBMS vendor to aggressively add object-relational functionality, doing nothing is a plausible option in this category. However, under the direction of Rick Cattell at Sun Microsystems, the OODB vendors have formed a consortium, called the Object Database Management Group (ODMG), with a charter to construct standards for the O vendors. The ODMG has a draft standard for object services, which includes a query language, OQL. It remains to be seen how aggressively the various O vendors will move to implementing OQL. Like SQL-3, OQL is a "moving target," and the subject of substantial technical development.

12.2 *Strategy 2: Rewrite a Relational Engine from Scratch*

The second alternative available to a relational vendor is to rewrite its DBMS from scratch. This is innately appealing because it allows designers a clean sheet of paper on which to craft a new system. Unfortunately, it is also highly risky for the following reasons:

- Writing several hundred thousand lines of fresh code is a complex, time-consuming task even under the best of circumstances. Many organizations have failed or been significantly late in delivering new systems because they underestimated the sheer amount of effort involved.

- In order to justify the venture, there is pressure to make the rewrite better than the current system in all ways. The new system must have all the functionality of the old system and offer the same or better performance on all commands the old system can do. In addition, it must promise dramatic new functionality. Because current relational engines have been tuned for several years to offer very high performance in transaction processing applications, the new system must also have this capability.

- The new system must be as reliable as the old system, or customers will not switch. As relational vendors have proved over and over again, it takes a long time to knock all the bugs out of new releases. Stabilizing a new code line appears to take at least a year, and often much longer.

- The new system must be compatible with the old system, or customers' applications will have to be converted to run with the new system. Faced with conversion to a new system, a customer may get itchy feet and begin to evaluate competing products. Obviously, vendors do not wish to give competitors an opportunity to erode their customer base.

- The old system required hundreds of man years of effort to get to its current state. It is psychologically difficult for management to discard this investment.

A rewrite is a risky and costly proposition; embarking on such a project is not a decision to take lightly. A new system will take years to complete. The experience of Digital Equipment Corporation (DEC) in this area comes to mind.

In the mid 1980s DEC began developing a "from scratch" DBMS, called RDB*, at its Colorado Springs facility. The project was kept completely separate from DEC's RDB group on the East Coast. The initial charter was to develop a relational engine for high-speed parallel hardware, a so-called software database machine. The system was to run on a loosely coupled collection of processors, an architecture that was similar to the Gamma prototype from the University of Wisconsin (Dewitt et al. 1990). This design required a complete DBMS engine for each network node as well as a distributed DBMS to manage the processing of multiple site queries.

A few years later the focus of RDB* shifted to that of a general-purpose distributed DBMS that could run on a network of conventional processors connected by commercial local area network (LAN) or wide area network (WAN) technology.

Within a couple more years the focus shifted again to supporting heterogeneous local DBMSs on the individual nodes of this network. This increase in scope required gateways to various foreign DBMSs.

Because the scope and direction of the project changed several times, by 1992 the group still had not delivered a product. Meanwhile, the RDB group on the East Coast was making consistent steady progress. Ultimately, DEC killed the RDB* project and incurred a financial write-off of many millions of dollars. A further exposition on the perils of this "cold turkey" development strategy is contained in Brodie and Stonebraker's book (1995).

12.3   *Strategy 3: Incremental Evolution*

The third option is to incrementally migrate an existing relational DBMS from its current state to an object-relational engine. Incremental migration of an existing system is advocated in Brodie and Stonebraker (1995) as the safest option for obtaining new functionality. Unfortunately, incremental migration will take a relational DBMS vendor several years to accomplish, most likely with a loss of market position.

The first vendor to adopt incremental evolution was Ingres Corp., which extended its relational engine in 1988 with base type extension and a rule manager, two of the four features that characterize an object-relational system. Although in both areas its initial offerings lacked needed functionality, Ingres made an early start toward object-relational functionality. Unfortunately, this incremental evolution largely stopped when Ingres Corp. was acquired by ASK in 1990. ASK, in turn, was recently acquired by Computer Associates and has now apparently adopted a gateway strategy to achieve object-relational functionality. This new strategy will be explored later in this chapter.

More recently, IBM has embarked on incremental evolution as their object-relational strategy. They have extended their UNIX relational engine, DB2/6000, to support base type extension and a rule system. This new system, DB2/6000 C/S, has just appeared. Again, IBM has chosen to implement two of the four tenets of an object-relational system, and they have done partial implementations of both. IBM has more work to do, which will presumably be forthcoming in subsequent releases.

In discussing IBM, it's important to carefully note that DB2/6000 C/S is one of at least four relational DBMSs available from IBM for various IBM operating systems. It has no common code with the flagship DB2 product, available for the MVS operating system. Do not assume that the object-relational strategy for DB2 (if one exists) is the same as the one for its UNIX sibling.

Lastly, Microsoft is apparently following incremental evolution. They are extending the Microsoft SQL server in place as well as rewriting portions of the system and exposing various internal interfaces. This project, internally called Nile, and more recently OLE/DB, is adding complex objects but not base type extension or inheritance to SQL. Look for OLE/DB functionality to appear in the marketplace over the next couple of years.

12.4   *Strategy 4: Write a Wrapper*

The fourth strategy available to a relational vendor is to write a *wrapper*. Basically, a wrapper is a simulation layer on top of a conventional relational engine. This simulation layer supports an object-relational API by mapping object-relational queries submitted by the user into relational ones, which are executed by a traditional relational engine. This wrapper architecture is shown in Figure 12.1.

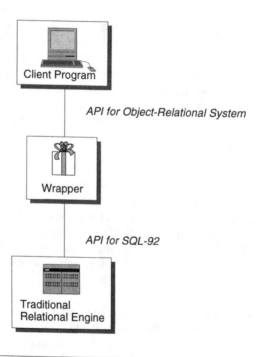

FIGURE 12.1 The Wrapper Architecture

Whenever there is a paradigm shift, a vendor with the old technology always has the option of writing a wrapper to support the new technology. This has been the case for years; for example, the IBM 370 line of computers supports an older technology, IBM 1401 programs, by simulating them on top of the 370. Closer to the DBMS space, Cullinet was the dominant vendor in the early 1980s with the then dominant technology (CODASYL). A new paradigm appeared (relational systems), and Cullinet decided to employ the wrapper technology to support it by writing a simulator for the relational model on top of CODASYL, called IDMS-R.

Hewlett-Packard has also adopted the wrapper strategy. It has written an object-relational DBMS wrapper, called Open ODB. Open ODB is implemented as a wrapper on top of Allbase, the HP relational DBMS. In fact, HP has more recently retargeted Open ODB to run on top of Oracle (renamed Odapter), so that it is now a wrapper for two different relational DBMSs.

Wrappers are just as appealing in the 1990s for vendors as they were for Cullinet in the 1980s. They allow a vendor with the old technology to quickly construct an implementation of the new technology. Then, over several years, the vendor can migrate its old engine by adding new function, changing the wrapper at each step to take advantage of whatever functionality is currently available in the underlying engine. Over these years of migration, the wrapper can insulate the user community, and eventually, it can be discarded when the vendor has native support for all wrapper functionality.

The problem with wrappers is poor performance on certain applications. To illustrate, consider the following object-relational table:

```
create table emp        (
                        name      varchar(30),
                        location  point,
                        resume    document,
                        friends   setof (ref (emp)));
```

This table contains a row for each employee in a given company and records the employee's name, home address, resumé, and a collection of references to the employee's friends. This table might be subjected to the following SQL command:

```
select name
from emp
where contained (location, circle ('0,0',2))
and wants (resume) = 'marketing'
and friends.name = 'Joe';
```

This query retrieves the names of employees who live inside a circle of radius two miles around the origin of the coordinate system, who want a marketing job, and who have a friend named Joe. If the function, *wants*, is registered with Illustra and the 2-D Spatial DataBlade module is installed, then the above query is legal in Illustra SQL.

Now consider the implementation of this query using a wrapper. Because point, document, and setof (ref(emp)) are not data types in SQL-92, the wrapper must actually create an SQL-92 table (or tables) with different types. As shown in Figure 12.2, the wrapper could choose to represent the data types as follows:

```
create table emp_92      (
                    name       varchar(30);
                    location   string
                    resume     blob
                    friends    varchar (100));
```

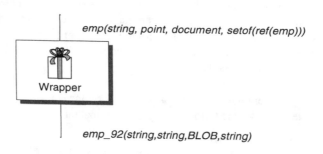

FIGURE 12.2   The Wrapper in Action

Here, the wrapper represents location as a string, say as a comma-separated list of two decimal numbers; resumé as a BLOB; and friends as a string, encoded, for example, as a comma-separated list of names of employees. Of course, there are many other ways that the wrapper can simulate the emp table, and there may be significant differences in performance between the various options.

In any case, the wrapper receives an object-relational query on the emp table and must actually run an SQL-92 query on the emp_92 table. Note that in the example above every clause in the predicate contains functionality not in SQL-92. Therefore, no clause is legal SQL-92, and as a result, the actual query run is

```
select *
from emp_92;
```

The entire query must now be performed in the wrapper, which means that the wrapper must have a second SQL parser, a second optimizer, and a second executor, all performing a simulation on top of a standard relational system.

In this example, this simulation will be extremely slow because a sequential search of all employees must be performed to satisfy the query. In contrast, a system like Illustra can use an R-tree access method to efficiently subset the employees on their spatial location, and thereby utilize indexing to do a lot less work. Additionally, the entire table must be moved out of the relational engine into the wrapper so that processing is not "close" to the data, incurring additional overhead.

12.5 *Strategy 5: Write a Gateway*

The fifth option is to use gateway technology, which connects an object-relational DBMS to a relational one. The required technology differs somewhat from traditional relational gateways as described below.

The standard relational gateway architecture is indicated in Figure 12.3. Here, you write an application using the API. Instead of processing the SQL commands in the user's program directly, the vendor inserts a relational *gateway* that maps the SQL commands submitted into the SQL dialect supported by a specific target system. Then, the gateway submits the command to the foreign system, interprets the returned results and error codes, and delivers the result to the user.

The gateway is a simulation layer that converts from one vendor's SQL to a second vendor's SQL. As such, the gateway is a special kind of wrapper whose purpose is the conversion between SQL-92 dialects. Of course, the gateway must also translate error messages and output data back from the foreign system. The architecture in Figure 12.3 is used by essentially all relational vendors to support access to foreign systems. Currently, most vendors have extensive collections of gateways to the popular foreign DBMSs.

Gateway technology can also be used by an object-relational DBMS vendor to support data in foreign DBMSs. At the current time, the main interest of object-relational vendors is in gateways to relational products. Figure 12.4 shows a simplification of the architecture being followed by most of these vendors. Suppose you have the following emp_R table stored in a relational system:

```
create table emp_R(
            name       varchar(30),
            salary     int,
            startdate  date);
```

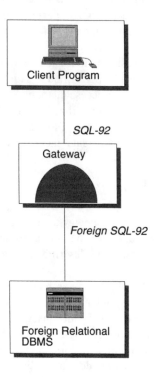

FIGURE 12.3   Relational Gateway Architecture

And suppose you want to run the following query:

```
select name
from emp_R
where salary = 10000
and vesting(startdate) > 0.6;
```

In this case, the query cannot be translated into SQL-92, because the second clause contains a user-defined function, *vesting*. Some of the query must be internally processed by the object-relational engine, in particular the following clause:

```
vesting(startdate) > 0.6
```

The remainder of the query,

```
select name
from emp_R
where salary = 10000;
```

can be translated by the gateway into the dialect of SQL used in the foreign vendor's system. As a result, your query must be processed by the object-relational engine and decomposed into two parts, one part to be done locally and one part to be shipped through the gateway to a foreign system. As a result, the gateway cannot be at the API level, as was noted in Figure 12.3. Instead, it must be internal to the object-relational system, and the architecture of Figure 12.4 results.

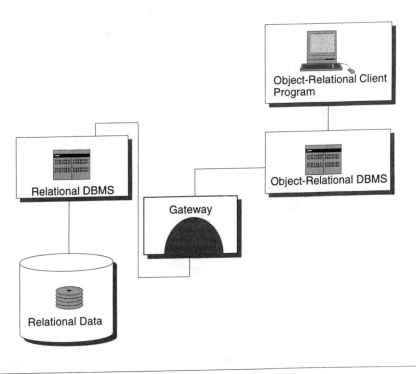

FIGURE 12.4   The Object-Relational Gateway

One interpretation of Figure 12.4 is that the object-relational engine plus the gateway implement the wrapper architecture from Figure 12.1. Thus, a relational vendor could partner with an object-relational one to quickly implement a wrapper.

In fact, the actual architecture used by the object-relational vendors is somewhat more general and is shown in Figure 12.5. Suppose you have an existing application managed by a relational DBMS. For example, you might have the above emp_R table with existing client programs. To this table, you might want to add two fields, location and picture, to form the following table:

```
create type employee_t(
                name        varchar(30),
                salary      int,
                startdate   date,
                location    point,
                picture     text);

create table emp of type employee_t;
```

Unfortunately, location and picture are not SQL-92 data types and cannot be easily managed by a relational DBMS. One option is to convert the application from a relational DBMS to an object-relational one to accommodate these extra fields. However, this requires substantial application maintenance, which would be resisted by the customer. A better option is to leave the relational data where it is and then to put the object-relational data in an object-relational system as noted in Figure 12.5. The relational system stores the table, emp_R, while the object-relational system stores

```
create table OR_internal(
                name        varchar(30),
                location    point,
                picture     ext);
```

Furthermore, the table you need can be declared as the following view:

```
create view emp_OR as
select e.*, i.location, i.picture
from emp_R  e, OR_internal i
where e.name = i.name;
```

This view creates a join between emp_R stored in a relational system and OR_internal stored in an object-relational one. Using this approach your current applications can continue to use the relational API without any dislocation, as shown in Figure 12.5. Furthermore, you can utilize the object-relational API for more general commands.

To implement the architecture of Figure 12.5, you need to be able to declare to the object-relational system that emp_R is a *foreign* table not stored by the local object-relational storage manager, but instead accessed through a gateway.

Using this architecture, you have available the full power of the object-relational engine to manipulate the emp_OR table. For example, you can submit the following query:

```
select name
from emp_OR
where salary > 5000
```

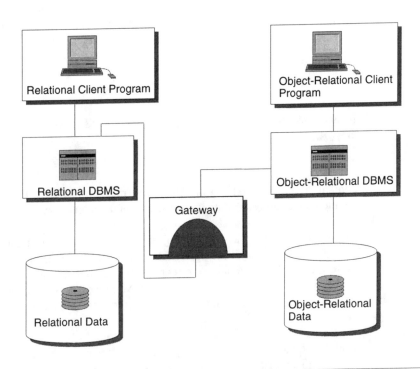

FIGURE 12.5 A Real Object-Relational Gateway Architecture

```
and vesting(startdate) > 0.6
and contained(location, circle ('0,0', 1))
and beard(picture) = 'gray';
```

Using standard view techniques, the object-relational engine transforms this query to

```
select name
from emp_R e, OR_internal i
where e.salary > 5000
and vesting(startdate) > 0.6
and contained(i.location, circle ('0,0', 1))
and beard(i.picture) = 'gray'
and e.name = i.name;
```

This is a conventional object-relational query that can be processed by the parser, optimizer, and executor in the standard way. During execution, the portion of this query that can be processed by the relational system, namely,

```
select name, startdate
from emp_R
where salary > 5000;
```

is forwarded to the relational engine for execution. The remaining predicate on emp_R,

```
vesting(startdate) > 0.6
```

contains a user-defined function. This clause must be solved by the object-relational engine after appropriate data is returned through the gateway.

In summary, the gateway from an object-relational DBMS to a relational one must be inside the executor of the object-relational engine, so that clauses that can be performed by the relational engine can be sent through the gateway, while ones that cannot are performed on the returned data. Moreover, data that cannot be easily modeled in a relational system should be stored locally inside the object-relational storage manager.

Both Illustra and UniSQL have implemented gateways with the architecture of Figure 12.5 to a variety of relational systems. They offer this functionality in order to support a *migration path* from relational systems to object-relational ones for users who have a deployed relational application. In time, you could expect to migrate complete applications onto the object-relational API. When that happens you can move all your data into the object-relational system, discard the gateway, and unhook the relational system. Of course, this might occur in several steps and perhaps over a substantial number of years.

A gateway from an object-relational system to a relational one is a good strategy for object-relational vendors; gateways provide you with a migration path to the newer technology without having to dislocate your existing application.

It is also possible for a relational vendor to utilize this strategy to quickly achieve object-relational capabilities. For example, Computer Associates has formed a relationship with Fujitsu, which markets an object-relational DBMS called ODB II. Fujitsu is writing a gateway from ODB II to CA-Ingres, and Computer Associates is actively marketing this partnership.

Although this section discusses gateways at the SQL level, it is possible that Fujitsu and CA-Ingres will interface ODB2 to CA-Ingres at a lower level. If this happens, then Fujitsu and CA-Ingres will be implementing the same architectural option

Tandem has choosen—namely, gluing an object-relational engine to a relational storage manager. For details, check with vendor announcements.

Of course, the disadvantage of gateway technology is poor performance. If you implement Figure 1.2, then the gateway plus the object-relational engine are really another kind of wrapper, and your gateway will have the same problems as any wrapper solution.

The architecture of Figure 12.5 is better, because some of the data is "native." However, any query that goes through the gateway will entail

- Translation of the outbound query by the gateway
- At least two messages between the gateway and the relational DBMS
- Copying all of the returned data from the foreign system to the object-relational one
- Possibly reformatting the copied data into the type system of the object-relational engine

Because of these limitations, gateways tend to be slow. This architecture will offer lower performance than a native implementation of an object-relational engine.

12.6   Strategy 6: An Object-Relational Top on a Relational Storage Manager

A relational DBMS is typically architected to run on top of a storage manager. This code module provides the following functionality:

- scans over tables
- index scans over tables using a B-tree index
- locking
- crash recovery
- page management

On top of this system, a parser, optimizer, and executor are crafted. This architecture was popularized by System R, the early IBM Research relational system from the 1970s, and is illustrated in Figure 12.6. Certain object-relational systems, such as Illustra, also use this basic two-level architecture.

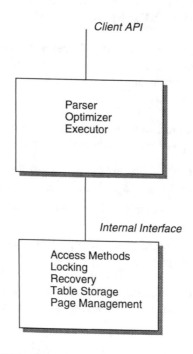

Client API

Parser
Optimizer
Executor

Internal Interface

Access Methods
Locking
Recovery
Table Storage
Page Management

FIGURE 1.4   Typical Relational Architecture

Tandem has elected to obtain object-relational functionality by "gluing" the Illustra "top half" onto the Tandem nonstop SQL "bottom half." At first glance, this is not an obvious solution. After all, what is the point of replacing the Illustra storage manager with a second one designed for the Tandem relational DBMS? The answer is simple: the Tandem storage manager supports nonstop operation through the unique Tandem process pair model, and it partitions tables over disks attached to multiple machines in a Tandem multiprocessor system. Neither feature is present in the Illustra storage manager. Therefore, Tandem has elected to employ the best features of each system to create an object-relational engine that will run well on the Tandem architecture and support nonstop operation.

Because the two storage managers have similar functionality, the "glue" required to match the pieces is not insurmountable and does not appear to present a performance problem.

This chapter has focused so far on the strategies that can be utilized by a relational vendor who wants to construct object-relational capabilities. The next two strategies are solutions for object-oriented DBMS vendors who want to add object-relational functionality.

12.7 *Strategy 7: Extend an Object-Oriented DBMS*

As noted in Chapter 1, most of the object-oriented DBMS vendors are selling "persistent languages," that is, systems tightly integrated with a specific programming language such as C++ or Smalltalk. They offer a runtime system in the same address space as the user's program, thereby giving up security for high performance. So far, most vendors have chosen to focus on the lower-right quadrant of the two-by-two matrix.

Most of the efforts of the ODMG (see page 147) have centered around standards for integrating persistent objects with C++ and Smalltalk (standards that are appropriate for the lower-right quadrant of the matrix). However, they have also specified a query language, OQL, for object databases. OQL has features in common with SQL-3; consider it as an alternate candidate for standardization for upper-right quadrant systems.

There are two possible future outcomes in this arena:

- OQL and SQL-3 will be rolled together into a single standard.
- OQL will be "buried" by SQL-3.

The forces pushing SQL-3 (IBM and Oracle) are much stronger than those pushing OQL. Therefore, expect SQL-3 to win in the marketplace. This outcome has nothing to do with the technical merits of either standard. It is simply a matter of the size of the "elephants" who are pushing SQL-3.

In any case, the O vendors have committed to working toward OQL systems, which requires the following steps:

1. Implement an SQL parser.
2. Implement an SQL optimizer.
3. Implement an execution engine for the resulting plans.
4. Bind the result onto their current runtime storage systems.
5. Decide to ignore (or do something) about the absence of security.

This list will take a fair amount of work to complete, since it specifies most of an object-relational DBMS. Object-oriented DBMS vendors will be busy for a while getting this much code to industrial-strength operation. Additionally, most of the O vendors currently execute methods (user-defined functions) on the client side of a client-server interface and perform static linking when the DBMS is installed. Thus, their architecture builds in some of the undesirable features discussed in Chapter 2. Fixing these problems requires still more work.

O vendors also have a dilemma concerning security. In the object-relational segment of the market, security is frequently mandatory. But object-oriented systems are focused on the lower-right quadrant and have no security requirement. The natural way for an O vendor to construct object-relational capabilities is with an extension of its current architectures, and thereby continue to have no security. Re-engineering a system to include security is a substantial job.

All the O vendors are small companies. It is difficult for these players to focus a critical mass of resources on two different segments of the DBMS marketplace. Expect most of them to pay lip service to the object-relational space and to only slowly add OQL implementations. Moreover, expect most of them to continue to ignore security and to have poor optimizers. An exception to this statement is O2, which has a rather advanced query capability.

There is, however, at least one object-oriented DBMS vendor that has adopted a different strategy, as you will see in the following section.

12.8   *Strategy 8: Glue an Object-Relational Engine onto a Persistent Language*

It is possible to interface an existing object-relational DBMS onto a persistent language. For example, UniSQL is structured with an internal interface that is close to a persistent language. In other words, it is possible to remove the UniSQL "bottom half" and interface the remaining "top half" onto an object-oriented DBMS. In fact, UniSQL and Versant have a partnership to do exactly this. In this way, Versant gets an object-relational query system quickly and can concentrate on its core business in the lower-right quadrant. For applications that have portions in both the upper-right and lower-right quadrants, this may be an attractive solution. Of course, static linking, client-side activation of functions, and security continue to be problems for this architecture, as they were for the previous architecture.

In a sense, this architecture is analogous to that described in Section 12.6. Relational vendors can use their "bottom half" with an object-relational "top half" that has a compatible storage manager. Object-oriented DBMS vendors can use their existing systems as a "bottom half" with an object-relational "top half" that has a compatible persistent language interface.

12.9 *Summary*

Table 12.1 reviews many of the vendors and their strategies for moving to an object-relational system. Also shown are the issues involved in each strategy.

TABLE 12.1. Strategies for Object-Relational DBMS Conversion

Strategy	Issues	Vendors
Evolve the system.	Safer, but time-consuming. Best single-vendor strategy.	IBM, Microsoft
Create a wrapper.	Possible performance loss.	Hewlett-Packard
Make a gateway.	Possible performance loss. But enables vendor to deliver market-ready product quickly.	Computer Associates
Glue an object-relational engine to a relational storage manager.	Good strategy, if performance is not compromised.	Tandem
Extend an object-oriented system.	Time-consuming, inherent security problems.	Most O vendors
Glue an object-relational engine to a persistent language system.	Good strategy, if performance is not compromised.	Versant

CHAPTER 13

Multi-Quadrant
Problems

This chapter discusses *hybrid* DBMS applications—problems that have characteristics of more than one quadrant in the DBMS matrix introduced in Chapter 1 and illustrated in Figure 1.1.

As you will recall, this is how the matrix is used to classify DBMS problems:

- The lower-left quadrant of the matrix requires no searching on simple data and is best served by file systems.
- The upper-left quadrant requires queries on simple data and is the domain of business data processing. It is well served by relational DBMSs.
- The lower-right quadrant requires support for complex data but not queries. This box is well-supported by object-oriented DBMSs.
- The upper-right quadrant requires queries on complex data and is best supported by object-relational DBMSs.

The matrix is a useful tool for classifying a DBMS problem and deciding which technology should be used to solve the problem. But what do you do if parts of your application fit into more than one quadrant?

This chapter discusses two such examples, a video service application and an insurance industry application, and explains why they are multi-quadrant applications. Then, Chapter 14 presents solutions for multi-quadrant applications.

13.1   *A Video Service Application*

Consider a cable television service that delivers movies on demand to people's homes. Through this service, customers can choose a video at any time and then play it through their set-top cable box on their television. The service offers movie previews for customers who want to sample a movie before ordering it. The service also maintains an on-line catalog of movie reviews that can be browsed by viewers who want a critical opinion of movies. Finally, because this service specializes in international films, it offers its customers the ability to identify films by their location of filming, for example, Cape Breton Island in Nova Scotia.

Assuming that an object-relational DBMS is available, the following tables are appropriate to support this application. The first table stores the video for each movie along with assorted attributes of the movie.

```
create table movie (
                mid          oid,
                mname        varchar(30),
                date         date,
                category     varchar(30),
                studio       varchar(30),
                stars        setof (varchar(30)),
                supporters   setof (varchar(30)),
                length       int,
                contents     mpeg);
```

The movie table contains an identifier for each movie, its name, the date it was released, the category of film (action, mystery, etc.), the studio that produced the film, the stars and supporting actors and actresses in the film, the running time of the movie in minutes, and finally the contents of the video in MPEG format. There is one row in movie for each available film supported by the service. The cable service projects that it will eventually need to support thousands of films.

The second table stores previews of films as follows:

```
create table preview (
                mid          ref(movie),
                length       int,
                contents     mpeg);
```

In preview, a reference is stored to the movie in the movie table that each preview describes, along with the length of the preview and its contents in MPEG format.

The third table stores reviews of movies for customers to browse:

```
create table review(
                    mid           ref(movie),
                    reviewer      varchar(30),
                    affiliation   varchar(30),
                    rating        rating_type,
                    review        document);
```

Each review describes a particular movie, identified by an mid, and contains the name of the reviewer and media affiliation (for example, the *New York Times*). Additionally, each reviewer uses a rating system to describe a film (three stars, thumbs up or down, excellent, and so forth). For each review, the rating given to the film by the reviewer in the reviewer's specific rating system is stored. This requires a new data type, rating_type, capable of storing a value from the rating system of any reviewer. The actual text of the review is also stored.

The last table describes the locations where each movie is filmed. This information typically appears in the credits at the end of the film and is stored in the following table:

```
create table location(
                    mid        ref(Movie),
                    location   point);
```

Here, location is coded as a (latitude, longitude) pair that indicates the coordinates of filming location. For simplicity, movies that are filmed in more than one place have multiple entries in this table.

If this application is implemented on a relational DBMS, then the schema needs to be changed somewhat because of the absence of references, sets, and user-defined types:

```
create table movie_R (
                    mid        int,
                    mname      varchar(30),
                    date       date,
                    category   varchar(30),
                    studio     varchar(30),
                    length     int,
                    contents   blob);
```

```
create table star_R (
                        mid        int,
                        star       varchar(30));

create table supporter_R (
                          mid              int,
                          supporter        varchar(30));

create table preview_R (
                        mid        int,
                        length     int,
                        contents   blob);

create table review_R (
                        mid              int,
                        reviewer         varchar(30),
                        affiliation      varchar(30),
                        rating           int,
                        review           blob);
```

In this version of the schema, identifiers must be created for all movies, and it is assumed they are integers. In addition, the movie table must be decomposed into three tables storing movie information, star information, and information about supporters. Furthermore, the contents of the movie must be stored as a BLOB, since MPEG is not a data type in a relational system. In the review table, rating must be simulated using an existing data type, such as an integer. The same comment applies to the review field, which is assumed to be a BLOB. (Because it requires a fair amount of user-level logic, this example does not attempt to model the location information.)

With these tables in place, a collection of queries that naturally fall in three of the four boxes in the application diagram can be described.

A Lower-Left Quadrant Example

The most common operation in a video service is for a customer to request the service to play a selected movie. This query can be expressed in standard SQL as follows:

```
select contents
from movie
where mname = 'desired-name';
```

Although this is certainly a legal statement in Illustra SQL and in a relational system, video services use a file system to implement this functionality today. Specifically, if all you need to do is identify an object by name and then retrieve the entire object onto a network connection for delivery to a customer, you hardly need a DBMS. In fact, this command can be thought of as the video equivalent of the text editor operation used as an example in Chapter 1, where the application reads an object by name in its entirety and then operates on it.

In the commercial marketplace all providers of video-on-demand services use a file system to implement this functionality. Specifically, Silicon Graphics used its file system in the Orlando, Florida, video-on-demand pilot system trials. Moreover, the Oracle video server is marketed as a DBMS solution, but in fact is a high-speed file system with a custom application delivering bits to network connections. The Oracle DBMS is used only to store the attribute data about each movie. Microsoft has implemented a high-performance file system for video, called Tiger. Again, there is no DBMS involvement in this functionality. Playing a video is a lower-left quadrant application, one that requires no searching on simple data and that is best served by a simple file system.

Upper-Left Quadrant Examples

The following two examples fit into the upper-left quadrant of the matrix. An easy query is to find the running time of *Dirty Harry*, which is coded as follows in a relational engine:

```
select length
from movie_R
where mname = 'Dirty Harry';
```

As a second example, suppose you want to find the action movies starring Clint Eastwood filmed in 1993. This can be expressed in Illustra SQL as follows:

```
select mid
from movie
where category = 'action' and
stars contains 'Clint Eastwood' and
date >= '1993-01-01' and
date < '1994-01-01';
```

Similarly, it can be expressed in relational SQL as

```
select M.name
from movie_R M, star_R S
where M.category = 'action' and
M.mid = S.mid
and S.star = 'Clint Eastwood' and
M.date >= '1993-01-01' and
M.date <= '1994-01-01';
```

Although it is a little easier to express in an object-relational system, this query can be readily expressed in a relational engine. Because it entails only simple data types it can be considered an upper-left quadrant query. Additional upper-left quadrant queries include

- What is the number of movies in the video service that star Sean Connery?
- Did Clint Eastwood star in movies from multiple studios during the 1980s?

Both of these example queries are readily expressible in either a relational system or an object-relational system. In some cases, the object-relational query is simpler, while in other cases, the two expressions are the same. These example queries fall in the upper-left corner of the matrix.

Upper-Right Quadrant Examples

The examples in this section lie in the upper-right quadrant. As a first example, suppose you want to find the movies that movie critics Siskel and Ebert like. This is expressed in Illustra SQL as follows:

```
select  deref (mid).mname
from review
where reviewer = 'Siskel and Ebert'
and liked (rating);
```

In this example, a user-defined function on the rating_type called *liked* is required. This function will return true if the movie got a rating that could be quantified as the critic liking the movie. Without a function, *liked*, this functionality must be provided in a user program. Thus, in a relational system, you can find the movies reviewed by Siskel and Ebert in SQL but then you must perform the rest of the query in a user program.

The next example is even more difficult for a relational system. Suppose you want to find action movies that contain the word "fabulous" in at least one of their reviews. This is expressed in Illustra SQL as follows:

```
select deref (mid).mname
from review
where contains (review, 'fabulous')
and deref (mid).category = 'action';
```

In this case, a function, *contains*, examines the text of a review for the word "fabulous." In Illustra, there is a *contained* function that is defined in the Document DataBlade module. Moreover, instances of the document data type have a keyword index built on the stems of all words that are not on a stop list that appear in the document. This keyword index uses a variant of a B-tree access method to store this word index. This means that the reviews that contain the word "fabulous" can be found very rapidly. There is no such functionality in a standard relational DBMS to provide similar indexing for BLOBs. As a result, the user must write substantial user-space logic to implement this functionality.

The last example in this section is the most difficult query of all for a relational system. Suppose you wish to find the movies that were shot within 50 miles of San Francisco during 1994. This is readily expressed in Illustra SQL as

```
select deref (mid).mname
from location
where year (deref (mid).date) = 1994
and distance (location, make_point ('San Francisco')) < 50;
```

To implement this query in a relational system, you must implement geographic locations (somehow) in user logic and then be able to efficiently find the points within a 50-mile radius of a specific city. On the other hand, this functionality is directly available in the Illustra 2-D Spatial DataBlade module.

The video service application contains queries that fit in three of the four quadrants of the DBMS classification matrix. There is no single system that performs well on all aspects of the video service problem. In this case, you are left with a dilemma concerning which kind of a DBMS to utilize. The remainder of this chapter gives a second example application with the same dilemma.

13.2 *An Insurance Application*

Consider a conventional insurance application containing customer and claims information:

```
create table customer_R (
                  cname          varchar(30),
                  caddress       varchar (40),
                  last_premium   money,
                  date_paid      date,
                  start_year     int);


create table claim_R (
                  cname    varchar(30),
                  amount   int,
                  date     date);
```

This sort of information is easily represented in a traditional relational system. For example, whenever a customer makes a premium payment, a transaction must be posted to the customer table updating the last_premium and date_paid fields. Similarly, whenever a claim is made, an insertion must be made to the claim table. In an industrial-strength version of this example there would be many more fields and additional transaction types. These would include sending out payment notices to customers and commission checks to agents. Additionally, this database is accessible on-line by all of the insurance company's agents so that many transactions and inquiries are submitted from many terminals to a common database.

So far, this application is a conventional business data processing problem that fits in the upper-left quadrant. Most insurance companies have implemented such systems either on a relational DBMS or on some sort of legacy mainframe DBMS. Relational DBMS vendors have spent many years tuning their engines to perform well in these kinds of environments. Although object-relational engines can also handle this application, they have not been tuned to perform well when there are lots of users doing transaction processing. Therefore, a relational DBMS is the best system to handle this problem.

However, most insurance companies want to extend their traditional database with new information. What they really want are tables like the following:

```
create table customer (
                    cname           varchar(30),
                    caddress        varchar (40),
                    last_premium    money,
                    date_paid       date,
                    start_year      int,
                    location        point);

create table claim (
                    cname           varchar(30),
                    amount          int,
                    date            date,
                    police_rpt      image,
                    dented_car      image,
                    location        point);
```

Notice the geographic location of the home of each customer is added to the customer table. The location of the accident that each claim is associated with, along with the picture of the dented car and the scanned image of the police report, are also new in the claim table. With this extra information there are numerous things that an insurance company would be able to find out. For example, it would like to know which customers live within a mile of a site that has had a claim. Perhaps the company would like to assess an extra premium to customers who live close to an intersection with a high accident rate. This query is expressed in Illustra SQL as follows:

```
select  C.cname
from customer C, claim CL
where  distance (C.location, CL.location) < 1;
```

Further, suppose the insurance company has written an expert system that examines the picture of a dented car and guesses the amount of the associated claim. If this is a user-defined function, *Guess*, then the following query finds the claims that are suspicious in nature because they cost substantially more to fix than the expert system estimates:

```
select  cname
from claim
where amount  - Guess (dented_car)  > 3000;
```

Such queries are extremely difficult for a relational DBMS to perform and clearly belong in the upper-right quadrant. This is an example of an application that has a component in the upper-left quadrant and a component in the upper-right quadrant.

Basically, the application begins with a stable transaction processing problem. Over time this part of the application will grow at the rate that the customer base expands, perhaps at 10% per year. To this base will be added an ever-increasing collection of multimedia data types and their associated decision support queries. Such decision support queries will be used to identify fraudulent claims, hot spots of activity, repair shops that charge high prices, and so forth. Over time, this component of the application will grow very rapidly, and it is entirely upper-right quadrant activity. The end result is that this application will move quite rapidly from being mainly an upper-left quadrant application to being an upper-right quadrant application.

The cost of disks, main memory, and CPUs is decreasing at a rate of almost a factor of two per year—the hardware needed to process a given workload will be one-half as expensive next year as this year, and one-quarter the price in two years. At the same time, the insurance company transaction workload might well be growing at 10% per year. In effect, this workload is getting cheaper to execute at slightly less than a factor of two per year. Over time, the cost of the hardware required to support this component of the insurance application will decline into insignificance. On the other hand, the computation and storage demands of the multimedia decision support component are extreme. The bottom line is that the hardware optimization should shift to dealing with multimedia computation and storage instead of with the transaction workload. This effect can be summarized in the following three observations:

Observation 1. Business data processing databases are about to increase in size by three orders of magnitude as users put multimedia objects (video, audio, images, geography) into their databases.

Observation 2. The average byte will be video or image data (since these types are by far the largest ones). Unless users have a lavish hardware budget, the average byte will live on near-line storage. Tape or CD (compact disc) robots and stackers are expected to form the majority of the devices supporting such tertiary memory.

Observation 3. The average CPU cycle will be used for decision support queries on multimedia objects.

As a consequence of these observations, the transaction processing workload will drift into insignificance. Put differently, there are only two known workloads above 1000 transactions per second, United Airlines and American Airlines. All other workloads are lower, and most are under 25 transactions per second. To buy the hardware to support 1000 transactions per second requires little more than a shared-memory multiprocessor made up of commodity parts. Clearly SMP technology applied to personal computers will be the cheapest option. Running most any work-load can be done for under $100,000. If the $100,000 solution doesn't perform well enough, the best decision may well be to throw another $100,000 of hardware at the problem.

Thus, you can expect an increasing proportion of transaction processing problems to be solved using brute force. This means that having a staff of highly paid wizards in white lab coats hovering over a transaction processing machine to ensure its stable, high-performance operation will become a thing of the past.

CHAPTER 14

Solutions to Multi-Quadrant Problems

This chapter discusses possible solutions to the multiple-quadrant problems introduced in Chapter 13. These are problems that don't fit neatly into just one quadrant of the DBMS matrix.

Strategies for handling two-quadrant problems are presented first. In these scenarios, assume there is a DBMS for the primary quadrant where the user's application resides, and the user is faced with the problem of supporting the minority of his application, which falls into a second quadrant.

Table 14.1 lists the nine two-quadrant problems that are discussed in this chapter. In the table, the primary quadrant is on the vertical axis, while the secondary quadrant is depicted horizontally. (The diagonal in the matrix represents single-quadrant problems, which are not the focus of this chapter. Also, if the primary quadrant is in the lower-left quadrant, and a file system is employed as the primary storage system, then there is no obvious way to support other kinds of DBMSs. Therefore, the top row of the table is also not discussed.)

After treating several two-quadrant problems, this chapter looks at problems that have portions of an application in three quadrants.

TABLE 14.1   The Possible Options

Primary Quadrant \ Secondary Quadrant	Lower-Left *(File System)*	Upper-Left *(Relational)*	Lower-Right *(Object-Oriented)*	Upper-Right *(Object-Relational)*
Lower-Left *(File System)*	X	Not Discussed	Not Discussed	Not Discussed
Upper-Left *(Relational)*	14.1, page 176	X	14.6, page 179	14.8, page 180
Lower-Right *(Object-Oriented)*	14.2, page 177	14.4, page 178	X	14.9, page 181
Upper-Right *(Object-Relational)*	14.3, page 177	14.5, page 178	14.7, page 180	X

14.1 *Upper-Left Primary Quadrant DBMS with a Lower-Left Secondary Quadrant*

Assuming you have chosen a relational DBMS for your application, you need a way to deal with pieces of the application that access file objects. There are two strategies for dealing with this situation:

Option 1. You can implement file objects as BLOBs in a relational DBMS. Then, to access a file object, you use the relational DBMS interface to access the BLOB. Normal relational queries can be run against the remainder of the data in the relational DBMS.

This strategy stores all data in the DBMS; however, it offers poorer performance than if the data were stored in a file system. The reason for this performance degradation is that BLOB storage is typically slower than if a standard file system is used.

Option 2. A second strategy is to store file objects directly in the file system. Then, in the relational DBMS you can then store a character string, say, the full path name of the file, as an identifier for the object. In this way, the name of the file is stored in the DBMS, and it can be retrieved as the result of a query. Then you can simply open the file and read the object at high speed. In this way, you can split the data between a file system and a relational DBMS. This approach requires some application logic because you must get a file name from the DBMS and then manually interact with the file system to read the object.

14.2 Lower-Right Primary DBMS with a Lower-Left Secondary Quadrant

In this situation, there is an object-oriented DBMS as the primary DBMS and a need to support file access for part of the application. Because object-oriented DBMSs do not have BLOBs, option 1 (page 176) is not available. However, you can always implement the effect of BLOBs by constructing an object that is an arbitrary-length string of characters. It is also always possible to store the file data separately in a file system and then put file names in the object-oriented DBMS.

Thus, close analogies to both options 1 and 2 can be used. Both will give reasonable performance and you can decide which is best for your particular environment.

14.3 Upper-Right Primary DBMS with a Lower-Left Secondary Quadrant

It is not unusual to have an object-relational DBMS problem that requires file access for part of the application. There are three choices for solving this sort of problem, which are discussed below.

Option 1. You can construct a "file type" as a new base data type in the DBMS. This data type stores the bytes of a file object in an instance of the file data type. You can also implement any desired operations for this type. This data type will give you the characteristics of BLOBs from the relational discussion above.

Option 2. Alternatively, you can construct a data type that stores a value that is a file name and has the input routine store the actual bits in a file outside the DBMS. On output, the converse routine reads the bits and returns them to the user. This achieves the effect of storing file names in the DBMS and data storage directly in the file system. Application logic is simplified because the input and output routines for the data type perform some of the work.

Option 3. You can store file names in the object-relational DBMS and then manually store the bytes directly in the file system. This solution exactly mimics option 2 from the relational discussion above (page 176).

Thus, the object-relational engine has a superset of the options available in the relational engine.

14.4 *Lower-Right Primary DBMS with an Upper-Left Secondary Quadrant*

This case involves a lower-right quadrant DBMS and the requirement to run SQL-92 queries against it. Some of the O vendors now have SQL support in their systems, which enables this sort of operation. Unfortunately, the SQL offered is often less than useful in some situations. For example, few O vendors allow you to issue SQL update statements. It is entirely possible that the SQL from a lower-right quadrant system is not rich enough to satisfy your needs.

This sort of two-quadrant problem can be handled by using an object-relational system from one of the object-relational DBMS companies as a wrapper on top of an object-oriented DBMS. In this way, you can certainly run relational queries, which are a subset of object-relational ones, by presenting them to the wrapper. At least one O vendor (Versant) has a partnership with an object-relational vendor (UniSQL). In their product, UniSQL runs as a wrapper on top of Versant. Obviously, this alternative is also available to the user who has an object-oriented DBMS and requires object-relational queries.

If options discussed in this section are not possible, you will have to code your SQL command in persistent C++, an unpalatable alternative.

14.5 *Upper-Right Primary DBMS with an Upper-Left Secondary Quadrant*

This case is perhaps the easiest to deal with. Because SQL-92 is a subset of the language supported by an upper-right quadrant DBMS, you can simply utilize the primary DBMS to execute the upper-left quadrant queries. The only disadvantage to this tactic is that an upper-right DBMS will execute SQL-92 more slowly than a relational DBMS would.

The reason for mediocre transaction processing performance is that the object-relational vendors have not tuned their engines for these kinds of workloads. There is nothing to prevent them from doing the same kinds of tuning over time that the relational vendors have employed. After all, when relational systems were first introduced, they were considered slow on transaction processing workloads. Over time, they were tuned to do much better. Presumably the same performance curve will be climbed by the object-relational vendors.

The reason for marginally poorer performance on SQL-92 decision support workloads, relative to relational DBMSs, has to do with system architecture. Presumably a relational engine and an object-relational one will choose the same query plan to execute an SQL-92 query. Assuming that both systems store records in roughly the same way, then both systems will read roughly the same number of pages. However, the relational engine has type-specific B-trees while the object-relational one has generic B-trees. Because the object-relational DBMS is much more flexible, the B-tree code is fundamentally slower. And, because there is extra indirection in the B-tree code and elsewhere in the executor, an object-relational engine will consume more CPU time than its relational counterpart when executing a relational query plan. This results in a modest performance hit.

14.6 *Upper-Left Primary DBMS with a Lower-Right Secondary Quadrant*

In this case, a relational DBMS can be used to handle most of the application's needs, but a portion of the application requires storing complex data and accessing it through persistent C++. There are two strategies to deal with this situation, and neither of them is very elegant. Hopefully, future research and development will bring better solutions.

The first choice is to use a wrapper to simulate a lower-right quadrant system on top of an upper-left quadrant system. In this way, there will be relational tables accessed directly by the application through the relational DBMS. And there will be other tables that are used by the wrapper to simulate complex objects. Moreover, the wrapper supports some sort of persistence in C++. You are free to manually construct this wrapper or you can buy a commercial product. For example, Persistence, Inc. sells a wrapper with these characteristics for various relational DBMSs.

The problem with this approach is that the wrapper usually does not perform well. For example, if you are navigating in C++, then you will typically cause the wrapper to run one SQL query per navigation step. Unless very clever pre-fetching and cache management are employed, then the data required by the next navigation step are not in main memory at the time the application requires them and a query must be run to fetch them. Each pointer dereference (navigation step) in the wrapper-supported persistent C++ will probably cost several milliseconds, and your program will run orders of magnitude slower on the wrapper than on a transient C++ system or on a real object-oriented DBMS. Typically, the performance of the "O on top of R" wrapper is extremely poor.

The second alternative is not very encouraging either. Specifically, you can put your upper-left quadrant data in a relational DBMS and your lower-right quadrant data in a persistent C++ system. With this solution, you are running two DBMSs, an R system side-by-side with an O system.

The problem with doing this is that your database administrator has to administer two systems. Also, inevitably users will ask to perform joins between data in the two systems. (Users will want to ask upper-right quadrant questions.) Thus, what was a two-quadrant problem will turn into a three-quadrant problem.

The two primary choices for handling this situation are not very appealing. Perhaps future development will bring some better solutions.

14.7 *Upper-Right Primary DBMS with a Lower-Right Secondary Quadrant*

There are two plausible alternatives available in this situation. First, you can use an object-relational DBMS that has an internal interface corresponding to persistent C++. If the vendor exposes this internal interface, then you can code the lower-right quadrant commands against this internal interface and the upper-right ones directly against the API of the system.

The second solution is to provide a wrapper on top of an object-relational DBMS that simulates a persistent language. This option was discussed as an alternative to provide a persistent language on top of a relational DBMS, and the same option can be employed for an object-relational DBMS. Unfortunately, there are no commercially available wrappers that I know of which handle this situation. Perhaps such products will appear over time, as the market for object-relational DBMSs increases in size.

14.8 *Upper-Left Primary DBMS with an Upper-Right Secondary Quadrant*

There are three alternatives available for this situation. First, as discussed in Chapter 12, most of the object-relational vendors offer gateways to relational DBMSs. This architecture was illustrated in Figure 12.5 on page 157. In this case, relational queries can directly access the relational DBMS, while object-relational queries are processed by the object-relational engine and relational data is accessed through the gateway. This is an effective solution when the application is primarily in the upper-left quadrant but upper-right queries and data are an auxiliary requirement.

Alternatively, you can use a wrapper such as Hewlett-Packard's Odapter. This architecture was illustrated in Figure 12.1. Relational commands are processed directly by the relational engine, while object-relational queries go through the wrapper. A wrapper is a degenerate case of the gateway architecture indicated in Figure 1.3, in which there is no data stored directly in the object-relational storage manager.

Of course, either architecture has a performance problem when running object-relational queries against relational data because the wrapper or the gateway introduces significant overhead. However, as long as the minority of the workload is object-relational, this performance hit should not be too severe.

The third alternative is to wait for additional options to become available. As noted in Chapter 12, most relational vendors are actively working on some sort of object-relational strategy.

14.9 *Upper-Right Primary DBMS with a Lower-Right Secondary Quadrant*

The last case is the one where the primary DBMS is a persistent language and you need object-relational capabilities for part of your application. In this case, you can run the UniSQL/Versant system mentioned earlier in Section 15.4 or use the SQL available from your object-oriented DBMS. In effect, you have the same choices available as you do for the situation where relational access for an object-oriented DBMS is needed.

14.10 *Applications in Three Quadrants*

The techniques discussed at the beginning of this chapter can be used to extend any two-quadrant architecture with support for files. Thus, any two-quadrant solution can be extended in a straightforward way to the lower-left quadrant. Therefore, the main focus in the section is on problems that have aspects in all quadrants except the lower left.

The first solution is called a "one-DBMS" architecture in Figure 14.1. This figure shows a relational DBMS as the main storage system that directly processes relational commands. On top of this engine are two wrappers, one for O queries and one for OR queries. In this way, three kinds of queries can be processed by one DBMS and two wrappers. Figure 14.1 was drawn assuming the primary single DBMS is a relational system; however, analogous figures can be drawn for a primary DBMS that is object-oriented or object-relational. The problem with a one-DBMS strategy is that two of the three kinds of queries are processed by a simulator, and performance will suffer.

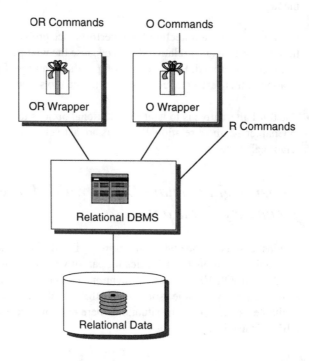

FIGURE 14.1   Example One-DBMS Architecture

A higher performance alternative is to use a "two-DBMS" strategy such as the design explored in Figure 14.2. Here, two DBMSs, a relational one and an object-relational one, are used. Some data is stored in each system, as noted. Moreover, relational queries are processed directly by the relational engine, and object-relational queries are processed directly by the object-relational engine. Of course, if an object-relational query requires relational data, it must fetch it through the gateway and a performance degradation will occur. Now, only one kind of command requires a wrapper. Figure 14.2 shows an O wrapper on top of the relational system.

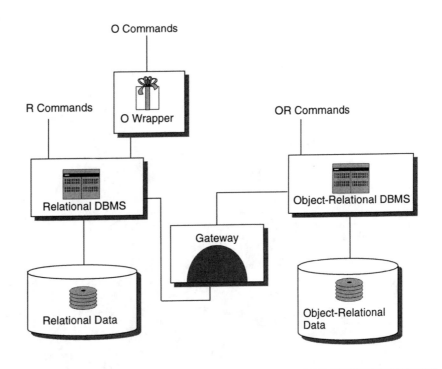

FIGURE 14.2   Example Two-DBMS Architecture

Again note that Figure 14.2 is just an example of a two-DBMS architecture. You can draw analogous figures for the other possible combinations of two DBMSs. The advantage of this architecture is that more of the user's application is processed directly by a DBMS, as opposed to going through a wrapper. This means that augmented performance should be available in a two-DBMS architecture relative to an architecture with a single DBMS. Of course, the downside is that a second DBMS must be purchased and maintained.

Although it is certainly possible to draw a three-DBMS architecture, it is not clear that you would be well advised to pursue this option. The complexity does not appear to be worth the potential further gain in performance, relative to a two-DBMS implementation.

CHAPTER 15

Database Design for Object-Relational DBMSs

Many users have a great deal of trouble with database design, and poor schema design is responsible for the failure of many applications. In an effort to shed some light on this vexing area, this chapter begins with a presentation of some basic relational database design concepts, and then extends those principles to object-relational database design.

15.1 Relational Database Design

Good database design is challenging even for SQL-92 databases. This section looks at the traditional algorithm for relational databases. This procedure discussed here can be found in any text on database design, such as Toby Teorey's well-known book (1994).

Most design products use an entity-relationship (ER) model to assist users with database design. The ER model was first popularized by Peter Chen (1976) and has found universal acceptance in database design, but is rarely used as the data model for an actual DBMS.

ER database design tools offer a "boxes and arrows" drawing tool that assists you in constructing a graphical ER diagram to represent your data. The basic construction process is the following:

1. Identify the *entities* of the application.

These are objects that have an existence that does not depend on other constructs in the application. Alternatively, they are objects for which a unique identifier is appropriate, as well as ones for which it is natural to create and delete. Employees, persons, departments, and automobiles are all natural entities.

An entity is associated with a box in the ER drawing tool. Typically the name of the entity is used to identify the box. The sample application in this chapter uses the entities employee and department, as shown in Figure 15.1.

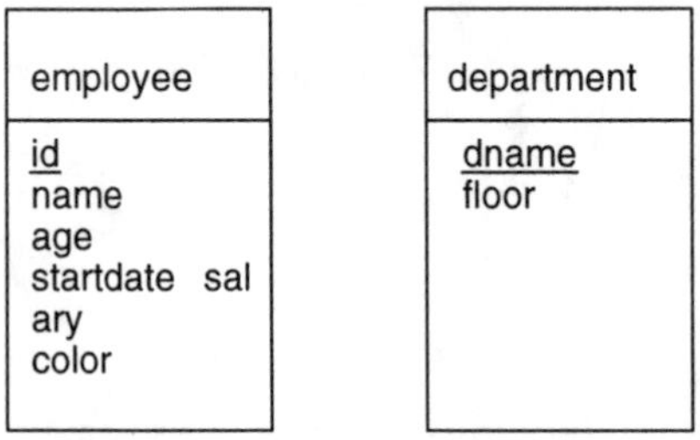

employee		department	
id		dname	
name		floor	
age			
startdate sal			
ary			
color			

FIGURE 15.1   A Typical ER Diagram

2. Identify the *attributes* of each entity.

Attributes are the fields that describe the entity. Relevant attributes for the employee entity might be name, startdate, salary, and hair color. Attributes for the department entity might be name and floor number. Each identified entity should have a data type.

Typically, the attributes of each entity appear inside the box containing the entity, or perhaps in a pop-up window activated by clicking on the box. Figure 15.1 shows each entity's attributes.

3. Give each entity a *unique identifier*.

It is reasonable that one of the attributes is a unique identifier. If the entity has such an attribute, then use it. Otherwise, assign another attribute to the entity that can hold a unique identifier. This can be a system-assigned object identifier (OID) or a user-assigned identifier.

The unique identifier is a primary key in relational terminology and is typically underlined in the ER diagramming tool. In Figure 15.1 dname is the primary key for department, while a new field, id, fills this need for employee.

4. Entities can participate in *relationships*.

A relationship is an association between two entities. For example "manages" is a relationship between an employee and a department, "works in" is a different relationship between an employee and a department, and "friend of" is a relationship between pairs of employees.

Relationships are indicated by drawing a line between the two entities that participate in the relationship. The three example relationships are shown in Figure 15.2.

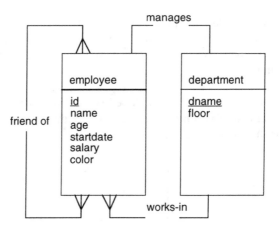

FIGURE 15.2   A Further Elaboration of the ER Diagram

For each relationship, indicate whether it is

- one-one: An entity on each side can only be related to one entity on the other side. Generally speaking, "manages" is a one-one relationship because an employee can manage only one department and a department is managed by only one employee.

- one-many: An entity on one side can be related to many entities on the other side, but an entity on the second side can only be related to one entity on the first side. For example, "works in" is a one-many relationship because an employee works in only one department but a department may have many employees working in it.

- many-many: An entity on each side can be related to many entities on the other side. For example, "friend of" is a many-many relationship.

The status of each relationship is drawn on the ER diagram. A line between the two entities indicates a one-one relationship, while a "crow's foot" at one end of the line indicates a one-many relationship. Crow's feet at both ends of the line indicate a many-many relationship.

5. Relationships can have *attributes*.

For each relationship, identify the attributes of the relationship. For example, works-in can have attributes "length-of-time" and "seniority status," while manages might have an attribute corresponding to the rating of the manager by his employees.

After you have completed these five steps, you have an ER diagram that represents your data. The complete ER diagram for the employee and department application is shown in Figure 15.3.

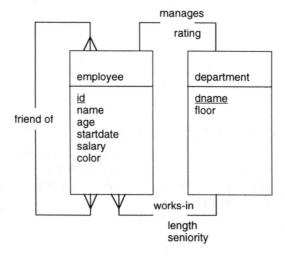

FIGURE 15.3   The Complete ER Diagram

The idea behind the ER drawing tools is that you will construct your ER diagram and then iteratively modify it until you capture the desired semantics of your application. When your diagram is adequate for your application, the ER tool typically can be instructed to generate a normalized collection of relational tables that correspond to the diagram. The algorithm to do this originally appeared in Wong and Katz (1979) and is repeated here.

1. Construct a table for each entity, containing all the attributes of the entity and having a primary key of the identified unique ID. The result of this step is the following two tables:

    ```
    employee(id,name,startdate,salary,color)
    department(dname,floor)
    ```

2. Construct a table for each many-many relationship containing the unique identifier for each side of the relationship along with the attributes of the relationship. The friend_of table shown below results from this step.

3. For each one-many relationship, add the unique identifier from the "one" side to the table corresponding to the entity on the "many" side, along with all the attributes of the relationship. As a result of this step, dname, length, and seniority are added to the employee table to capture the semantics of the "works in" relationship.

4. For each one-one relationship, add the unique identifiers from either side to the table for the other side, along with the attributes of the relationship. As a result of this step, id and rating are added to the department table to capture the "manages" relationship.

The end product is a collection of relational tables, which are normalized according to relational normalization theory, and a good relational database design. This collection is shown below:

```
employee(id,name,startdate,salary,color,dname,length,seniority)
department(dname,floor,id,rating)
friend_of(id_1, id_2)
```

Relational database design is straightforward. Simply follow the above procedures, either manually or with the help of an ER diagramming tool, and a good relational schema will result.

So why do users have so much trouble with database design? The next section looks at some reasons.

15.2   *Reasons for Problems*

There are at least six main reasons why people have a lot of trouble with database design:

1. Difficulty in tuning the schema
2. An unwillingness to iterate the schema
3. An unrealistic application design
4. Failure to load and test a large database early in the project
5. Difficulty in capturing the rest of the schema
6. Excessive focus on formal modeling of the application

Performance Tuning of the Schema

The first problem encountered in designing a database, schema tuning, is illustrated with the following SQL-92 query:

```
select name
from employee
where dname in
     (select dname
     from department
     where floor = 1);
```

This query finds the employees on the first floor by joining the employee table to the department table. If this query is very popular, you can accelerate the query by using appropriate indexing. In this case, building a B-tree index on floor provides appropriate acceleration. However, suppose the resulting query is still not fast enough to meet the response time requirements of the application.

The basic problem is that the query entails a join, and you may not be able to afford the response time that a join requires. One option is to buy faster hardware (an option usually resisted by users). A second option is to denormalize the two tables into something that is faster. In this case, you could combine them to produce

```
create table emp_dept(
                name        varchar(30),
                age         int,
                startdate   date,
                salary      int,
                color       varchar(10),
                dname       varchar(30),
                length      int,
                seniority   int,
                dname-2     varchar(30),
                floor       int
             id             int,
          rating            float);
```

In this case, the above query becomes

```
select name
from emp_dept
where floor = 1;
```

With a B-tree index on floor, this becomes an index scan of a single table, rather than a join. It will run much faster, because each potentially qualifying record is now in a single place rather than being spread over two tables as in the previous schema.

You can denormalize the tables in the schema for augmented performance on this query. Of course, this alteration also affects the performance of the rest of the application. More ominously, it replicates the floor number and name of each department in the employee record of each employee. If the floor number or name of a department changes, there is a serious integrity problem, in that all copies have to be found and updated. Additionally, the cost of this update goes up considerably relative to the previous schema we were using. The same comment applies to the replication of the information about the manages relationship.

You may have begun to notice that the choice of precisely which tables to denormalize is an art that requires good intuition and practice. This sort of schema tuning must be done by a "four-star wizard" who understands the complete application as well as the performance characteristics of the DBMS in use. Most application shops lack this level of expertise, and as a result, often create schemas that are not well optimized for the application.

If you don't have a four-star wizard on staff, then retain one as a consultant. A consultant can be extremely helpful in complex tasks of this sort. Although consultants typically are more expensive than regular employees, they are worth the expense.

Failure to Iterate the Schema

A second common problem is that developers are often unwilling to iterate the design.

It is essential that you recognize that schema design is an iterative process and that you will work on the design of a particular schema over and over again, as circumstances change. Moreover, whenever the schema changes, it will be necessary to perform at least some application maintenance. It is almost always a mistake to freeze the schema early in a project to avoid this maintenance. If the schema is wrong, the downstream headache is almost always worse than the incremental maintenance.

Put your best talent on schema design, and you will reap long-term rewards. Expect this task to consume significant resources, say 10–20% of the entire project budget, and don't skimp in this area. Make sure that there is at least one person whose only responsibility is this activity. Remember that it is never really finished.

Unrealistic Application Design

Unrealistic application design is another common problem. For example, an implementor often takes a fancy to some feature in a DBMS and then uses that feature to solve a multitude of other problems, without regard for whether it is a particularly good mechanism or not.

One example of a mechanism that can be overused is triggers. Clearly triggers are a powerful construct for enforcing business rules, and they should be used to advantage. However, there are business rules that are best enforced in other ways. For example, if you insist that an employee name is entirely alphabetic and has a capitalized first letter, then this is best enforced using the "edit check" facility of the 4GL being used to code the application. True, this can also be done using triggers, but the overhead is at least one order of magnitude higher. Forcing edit checks into the trigger system, will generate a serious performance problem and may endanger the success of the application.

Use good taste in deciding how and where to use any given DBMS feature.

Impossible Performance Goals

The fourth problem concerns impossible performance goals. A classic case is that of a large consulting company that agreed to build a transaction processing application for a customer who was a public service agency in an eastern state. In the specifications, the customer demanded two-second response time to 95% of the transactions in the application. The consultants proceeded to design the system and were most of the way through coding when they realized they were a factor of four away from meeting the response time specifications. The consultant's schema design was fine; however, the particular choice of hardware, application programming system, and DBMS was too slow to meet the needs of the application. Moreover, at that late date, there was essentially nothing that they could do to rectify the problem, and the project failed amid a flurry of lawsuits.

Obviously, the consulting company failed to heed a principal lesson of database design:

Load a large database early in the project and test mock-ups of the popular transactions for performance problems.

This activity identifies early in the project any performance problems you might face, so that you have time to take corrective action. If there is a single common mistake that application designers make, it is this one. The importance of this step cannot be over-emphasized.

Difficulty Capturing the Rest of the Schema

The fifth problem concerns capturing the rest of the schema. Clearly, there are a wide variety of business rules that must be enforced by the application. For example, in the employee and department example on page 189, it is reasonable to enforce the following business rule:

Every employee must work in a department.

There are a variety of ways to enforce this rule. For example, when an employee is added into a non-existent department, then all of the following actions are plausible:

- Refuse the insertion.
- Create a new department with the offered name.
- Put the new employee in the null department or a default department.

Similarly, when a department is deleted, the following actions are all possible:

- Refuse the deletion if there are employees in the department.
- Cascade the deletion; that is, fire the employees in the deleted department.
- Put the "orphaned" employees in the null department or a default department.

The user must specify which of these actions to take to enforce the condition. In general, a large number of business rules must be enforced in an application. A few examples now follow:

- Employees must have a positive salary.
- Employee names are a last name, followed by a comma, followed by a first name.
- A department can have at most 10 employees working in it.
- If a department has no manager, then the company president becomes the *de facto* manager.

The necessity of capturing these business rules poses additional problems in database design. Typically, it is difficult to get users to explain these rules in a way that application designers can understand. Moreover, if the system in question is replacing a legacy system, it is often the case that no human actually knows the required information and it is not documented anywhere. In this case, the only repository for the required information is the code of the legacy system. There are few exercises as costly and boring as decrypting antique code to figure out what it does.

Excessive Focus on Formal Modeling of the Application

The last problem is an excessive focus on formal modeling of the application and its resulting data. A typical instance of this is an application where a group of designers spend the first six months of their project examining the tools available in the commercial marketplace to support modeling the application and the schema. After a careful study, they determine that none of the tools meets their needs, and they propose to embark on building an in-house tool, a choice that clearly will take many additional months, if not longer, to build.

All too many teams spend all too much time on these ancillary activities, which do not contribute to getting the application built.

15.3 *Challenges in Object-Relational Database Design*

Because of its greater sophistication, database design in an object-relational DBMS is considerably more challenging than in relational systems. You face increased complexity in three areas:

1. Choosing from the multitude of options
2. Choosing procedural or data representation
3. Choosing rule or data representation

The following sections discuss the challenges posed in these areas.

More Options—More Potential Confusion

Clearly, an object-relational DBMS is a superset of a relational DBMS. All of the problems mentioned in the previous section also occur in an object-relational world. However, they are all more complex in an object-relational system.

For example, there are many more ways to deal with integrity constraints. It is possible to implement the employee and department tables mentioned above as well as the emp_dept table. In addition, you can implement dname in the employee table as a ref (department) type. You can also implement the works-in relationship by storing a set of references to employees in the department table. Furthermore, you could define your own data type that connected employee and department in some other way.

The same issue of increased complexity arises in denormalization. If you implement the employee and department schema, and then find that the SQL query is not fast enough, then you can denormalize to the emp_dept table. However, you can also implement dname in employee table as a ref (department) type. These both offer higher performance than the employee and department schema.

In addition, you can choose to implement a *floor(employee)* function that retrieves the floor of any employee when called. By itself, this will not increase performance. However, some object-relational systems allow you to specify that you want the result of a function to be precomputed and indexed. As a result, a B-tree index can be built on the result of the *floor* function. This index remains correct as employees change departments. Using function indexing, you can achieve very high performance.

In a good object-relational DBMS, you also have inheritance, base type extension, as well as a variety of complex objects available to use in schema design. It truly requires art and a lot of well-educated intuition to know how to use these concepts most effectively.

An object-relational database design contains all the hazards and correctives available in SQL-92 database design. In addition, because of the richness of the data model, database design is correspondingly more difficult.

Procedural versus Data Representation

The second problem concerns procedural versus data representation. Consider the birthdate and age of an employee. In a relational system, you must decide which one of these to store or, alternatively, to store both using a trigger for data consistency. Thus, you must decide on the representation of the data when there is more than one alternative.

However, in an object-relational system data can be encoded procedurally. As a result, it is possible to store either age or birthdate as a data field and then compute the other using a function.

Whenever procedural representation is utilized, you must decide whether to compute the corresponding functions on demand when they appear in a query (lazy evaluation) or to compute the function at data load time (eager evaluation). This performance and space trade-off must be understood and optimized by an object-relational database administrator.

Rule versus Data Representation

The third problem concerns the possibility of using rules to represent information. Return to the rule example from Chapter 7, which dealt with two employees, Jane and Mike, and the requirement that both have the same salary. In a relational system the obvious alternative is to store both salaries as data elements, and then enforce the rule with the following trigger:

```
create rule update_update  as
on update to employee.salary where current.name = 'Mike'
do update employee
            set salary = new.salary
            where name = 'Jane';
```

However, there is another way to accomplish the same goal in an object-relational DBMS, namely with a query-query rule:

```
create rule query_query as
on select to employee.salary where current.name = 'Jane'
do instead
        select salary
        from employee
        where emp.name = 'Mike';
```

Using this scheme, Jane's salary is never stored, but is computed when required using the rule. Clearly, both representations are available in a good object-relational DBMS. Unfortunately, making the choice between them requires substantial sophistication. There are two aspects to this choice.

First, the performance characteristics of the two choices are different. If Mike receives many raises, but it is rare to query for Jane's salary, then the trigger system will fire on each raise and propagate the new salary from Mike to Jane. However, queries that request Jane's salary are rare, and this overhead is wasted. Instead, one would prefer the second implementation where Jane's salary is computed by the rule when it is required in a query. Alternatively, if Mike receives few raises and Jane's salary is often queried, then the opposite choice is appropriate. An object-relational database administrator must understand the application and the performance envelope of the DBMS in order to intelligently make this trade-off.

In addition, there is a second somewhat devious aspect to the choice between these two rules-based alternatives, namely they have slightly different semantics. Suppose Mike is deleted from the employee table. In this case, using the trigger implementation, Jane's salary will be equal to Mike's salary at the time he left the company. In contrast, using the second implementation, Jane's salary will be null after Mike is deleted.

The object-relational database administrator must understand these subtle distinctions and decide which rule-based choice (or both) is usable.

15.4 *Summary*

Relational database design is difficult, and users struggle with this fact all too frequently. But object-relational database design is harder yet. The great wave of object-relational DBMSs may be threatened by the challenges real users will face when they try to create reasonable database designs.

Traditional database system vendors have done a clear disservice to the application community. In response to demand from sophisticated shops, they have created products with an enormous number of "tuning dials" in them. A sophisticated user (the four-star wizard) can use these dials to optimize a given application.

However, there are not enough four-star wizards to go around, and current systems have a built-in dependency on this level of sophistication. DBMSs will have to become much easier to use in the future. The course is clear; a system must be able to perform automatic tuning. An internal expert system can watch the workload being performed and then alter the tuning knobs automatically to achieve best performance. In addition, a second expert system can be built to explain to users the performance consequences of their design choices. This movement from human wizards to internal expert systems appears necessary in order for object-relational DBMSs to be truly usable by ordinary mortals—and thus to become broadly accepted in the business world.

CHAPTER 16

The Next Great Wave in DBMS Technology

This chapter begins with an overview of the book and concludes with a review of commercially available object-relational products. In this book you have seen why the object-relational DBMS's power to handle complex data will make it the next great wave in database technology. There are already signs that the object-relational database will eclipse relational technology as more and more of the major commercial vendors make a play for market share—and more importantly, as the user community begins to appreciate and require the features an object-relational database offers.

16.1 *Overview of the Book*

This book begins by pointing out the need for a new kind of DBMS that meets the requirements of the upper-right quadrant of the two-by-two application matrix. Chapters 2 through 7 define the four cornerstone *characteristics* of a good object-relational DBMS. These characteristics are

1. Base type extension
2. Complex objects
3. Inheritance
4. A rule system

The *features* required to support the four basic characteristics are outlined below:

1. Base Type Extension
   a. Dynamic linking of user-defined functions
   b. Client or server activation of user-defined functions
   c. Secure user-defined functions
   d. Callback in user-defined functions
   e. User-defined access methods
   f. Arbitrary-length data types

2. Complex Objects
   a. Type constructors
      - set_of
      - record of
      - reference
   b. User-defined functions
      - dynamic linking
      - client or server activation
      - securer user-defined functions
      - callback
   c. Arbitrary-length complex data types
   d. SQL support

3. Inheritance
   a. Data and function inheritance
   b. Overloading
   c. Inheritance of types, not tables
   d. Multiple inheritance

4. Rule System
   a. Events and actions are retrieves as well as updates
   b. Integration of rules with inheritance and type extension
   c. Rich execution semantics for rules
   d. No infinite loops

These characteristics and their detailed features provide a yardstick to evaluate any object-relational DBMS so that you can distinguish the pretenders from the real thing.

Chapters 8 through 11 discuss the construction of an object-relational DBMS and explore the requirements for implementing an object-relational parser, optimizer, and rule engine. Chapter 12 describes why major surgery is required on a traditional relational DBMS to extend its functionality to the four basic characteristics of an object-relational DBMS. Also discussed is the fact that considerable extension is required to turn an object-oriented DBMS into an object-relational one.

The strategies available to the existing commercial relational and object-oriented DBMS vendors are

- Do nothing.
- Rewrite a relational system from scratch.
- Incrementally evolve.
- Use a wrapper.
- Partner with an object-relational vendor using a gateway.
- Partner with an object-relational vendor by combining an object-relational top half with a relational bottom half.
- Extend an object-oriented DBMS with a top half.
- Partner with an object-relational vendor by using an object-relational top half with an object-oriented DBMS.

Chapter 12 identifies the vendors that utilize each of these strategies.

Multi-quadrant applications are the subject of Chapter 13. Discussed first are two examples of applications that exhibit characteristics of more than one quadrant in the two-by-two matrix. Because most DBMSs work well for applications inside their respective squares and poorly or not at all on other problems, multi-quadrant applications are not likely to be well-served by just one DBMS. Solutions available to users with multi-quadrant problems is the topic of Chapter 14.

The inherent difficulty involved with database design for object-relational applications is discussed in Chapter 15. Because of the challenges posed by object-relational database design, it is imperative that users begin to seriously develop and cultivate their database design and administration capabilities.

16.2   *Overview of the Object-Relational Marketplace*

A brief survey of the systems available in the commercial marketplace is next. The following tables indicate how well current systems comply with the characteristics and detailed features of a fully object-relational system. Also indicated is the architecture that each vendor is following. Only currently released systems are listed in the tables.

The following systems encompass at least some object-relational characteristics:

- DB2/6000 C/S
- Illustra
- CA-Ingres
- ODB II
- Odapter
- Omniscience
- UniSQL

The characteristics of these systems are summarized in Table 16.1. Each entry in this table is a "yes" or "no" indicating whether the system has the corresponding characteristic. For some systems it is difficult to ascertain if they have a specific characteristic. In this case, a "?" appears in the table.

There is one entry in the table that merits discussion. DB2/6000 C/S supports base type extension in that it allows new base data types and user-defined functions. However, operators for new types cannot be defined by a user. Instead, you must utilize the operators for one of the built-in types. For example, you can define Scottish name as a data type, but you are stuck with one of the SQL-92 collating sequences for the new type. As a result, B-trees cannot be used by the type, and "order by" in an SQL statement will work incorrectly. As a result, the table specifies "partial" for the presence of this characteristic in DB2/6000 C/S.

TABLE 16.1.   Characteristics of Object-Relational DBMSs

System	Strategy	Availability	Base Type Extension	Complex Objects	Inheritance	Rules
CA-Ingres	Evolution	1988	Yes	No	No	Yes
DB2/ 6000 C/S	Evolution	Now	Partial	No	No	Yes
Illustra	Native Implementation	Now	Yes	Yes	Yes	Yes
ODB II	Native Implementation	Now	No	Yes	Yes	?
Omniscience	Native Implementation	Now	No	Yes	Yes	?
Odapter	Wrapper	Now	No	Yes	Yes	Yes
UniSQL	Native Implementation	Now	No	Yes	Yes	Yes
Versant	Code Partnership	Late 1995	No	Yes	Yes	Yes

Systems that are fully object-relational must have all four characteristics of an object-relational DBMS given on page 199. As you can see, there are lots of pretenders—systems with much fewer than all four features.

Next, this chapter takes a more detailed look at the features displayed by the systems that are currently available in the marketplace. Tables 16.2 through 16.5 examine in turn the features of today's commercial systems. Each table deals with one of the four basic characteristics of an object-relational DBMS: base type extension, complex objects, inheritance, and rule systems.

Because it is difficult to get information from some of these vendors, a question mark indicates wherever there is an unknown parameter. Also, each table omits any vendor's system that does not have the characteristic at all. Only systems that are currently in production release are included. Lastly, the specific features of each product are likely to change rapidly. Therefore, check with each vendor for the most current information.

As Table 16.2 shows, there are a few systems that support base type extension. Moreover, the quality of some of the implementations leaves room for improvement. In the case of DB2/6000 expect future releases to fill in the missing features.

TABLE 16.2.   Features of a Fully Object-Relational DBMS in Support of Base Type Extension

Feature	DB2/60000 C/S	Illustra	CA-Ingres
Dynamic Linking	Yes	Yes	No
Client or Server Activation	No	Yes	No
Secure User-Defined Functions	Yes	No	No
Callback	No	Yes	?
User-Defined Access Methods	No	Yes	No
Arbitrary Length Data Types	Yes	Yes	?

On the other hand, Computer Associates has announced that their future object-relational strategy entails a partnership with Fujitsu and a gateway from ODB II to CA-Ingres. Because ODB II does not support base type extension, it is unknown whether CA-Ingres users can look forward to any improvement in features.

In Table 16.3, notice the poor support by many commercial systems for needed features of user-defined functions. However, because all of the systems listed are under active development, you can expect better compliance with the required features in future releases.

TABLE 16.3. Features of a Fully Object-Relational DBMS in Support of Complex Objects

Feature	Illustra	Omni-science	Odapter	UniSQL
Type Constructors				
set_of	Yes	Yes	Yes	Yes
record_ of	Yes	?	?	?
reference	Yes	?	?	?
User-Defined Functions				
Dynamic Linking	Yes	?	No	Yes
Client or Server Activation	Yes	No	No	No
Secure User-Defined Functions	No	No	No	No
Callback	Yes	?	?	Yes
Arbitrary Length Complex Data Types	Yes	?	?	?
SQL Support for Complex Objects	Yes	Yes	Yes	Yes

In Table 16.4 notice that commercial systems are much more compliant with inheritance features, than with the other object-relational characteristics.

TABLE 16.4. Features of a Fully Object-Relational DBMS in Support of Inheritance

Feature	Illustra	ODB II	Omni-science	Odapter	UniSQL
Data and Function inheritance	Yes	Yes	Yes	Yes	Yes
Overloading	Yes	Yes	Yes	Yes	Yes
Inheritance of Types, not Tables	Yes	?	?	?	No
Multiple Inheritance	Yes	Yes	?	?	Yes

Notice in Table 16.5 that most vendors have primitive trigger systems with impoverished semantics. Hopefully this state of affairs will improve in future releases.

TABLE 16.5. Features of a Fully Object-Relational DBMS in Support of Rules Systems

Feature	DB2/ 6000 C/S	Illustra	CA-Ingres	Odapter	UniSQL
Events and Actions are Retrieves as well as Updates	No	Yes	Yes	No	No
Integration of Rules with Inheritance and Type Extension	Type Extension Only	Yes	Type Extension Only	No	?
Rich Execution Semantics for Rules	No	No	No	No	No
No Infinite Loop	Yes	Yes	?	?	?

As the tables show, most vendors have very restricted compliance with a limited number of the object-relational characteristics. You could call them *pretenders* because they use the object-relational label but do not have a product that measures up.

Over the next several releases of these products, expect the compliance of the various systems to improve considerably. After all, many are relatively new systems. In addition, expect the number of object-relational systems to increase considerably with the release of additional object-relational systems from Informix, Microsoft, Oracle, and Sybase over the next few years.

One note of history is important at this point. In the 1970s the mainstream technology available in the marketplace was hierarchical and network systems. Relational technology was just being investigated in the research labs. Prototype systems were developed at the University of Toronto, the University of California, and IBM Research. In the 1980s relational technology came out of the research labs and into the commercial marketplace, causing a paradigm shift that displaced network and hierarchical systems as the dominant DBMS technology.

During the same decade, the research labs were hard at work on object-relational systems. Prototypes were constructed at the Microelectronics and Computer Corporation (MCC), the University of Wisconsin, IBM Research, and the University of California. In the 1990s these systems have come out of the research labs and will cause another paradigm shift to this technology. By the year 2000, expect that relational systems will be the new legacy systems and that the mainstream vendors will be marketing object-relational technology. Table 16.6 summarizes these observations.

TABLE 16.6.   A Lesson from History

Technology	1970s	1980s	1990s
Research Lab	Relational	Object-Relational	Not Yet Identified
Mainstream Commercial	Hierarchical and Network	Relational	Object-Relational
Legacy		Hierarchical and Network	Relational

16.3   *Summary*

Expect object-relational DBMSs to be the next great wave in database technology. This will be caused by the twin forces of

- rightward migration of business data processing applications
- new DBMS applications, especially multimedia Web-oriented ones

As a result of the first force, expect the majority of the $8 billion relational market to shift from the upper-left quadrant to the upper-right quadrant of the two-by-two matrix over the next decade. By the turn of the century the object-relational database will be the mainstream DBMS technology. By then, most of the major relational vendors will have a credible object-relational implementation and relational systems will become the new "legacy systems," joining hierarchical and network systems in this sunset category.

As users capture the 85% of information that is not yet computerized, there will be a huge new class of mostly upper-right quadrant applications, including digital library applications, electronic commerce, on-line catalogs, digital publishing applications, and asset creation and management—the second force behind the great wave.

The next great wave of the object-relational DBMS will be at least as dramatic as the last great wave, which saw relational systems replace network and hierarchical DBMSs in business data processing applications.

References

Brodie, Michael L., and Stonebraker, Michael. 1995. *Migrating Legacy Systems*: *Gateways, Interfaces, and the Incremental Approach*, Morgan Kaufmann, San Francisco.

Cattell, R. G. G. (editor). 1995. *The Object Database Standard: ODMG-93, Release 1.2*, Morgan Kaufmann, San Francisco.

Chen, Peter. 1976. "The Entity-Relationship Model—Toward a Unified View of Data," *ACM Transactions on Database Systems*, June.

Date, C. J. 1985. *An Introduction to Database Systems*, 4th ed., Addison-Wesley, Reading, MA.

Dewitt, David, et al. 1990. "The Gamma Database Machine Project," *IEEE Transactions on Knowledge and Data Engineering*, March.

Gray, Jim (editor). 1993. *The Benchmark Handbook for Database and Transaction Processing Systems*, Morgan Kaufmann, San Francisco.

Gray, Jim, and Reuter, Andreas. 1993. *Transaction Processing: Concepts and Techniques,* Morgan Kaufmann, San Francisco.

Gutman, A. 1984. "R-trees: A Dynamic Index Structure for Spatial Searching," *Proc. 1984 ACM-SIGMOD Conference on Management of Data*, Boston, June.

Hellerstein, J., and Stonebraker, M. 1993. "Predicate Pushdown for Expensive Functions," *Proc. 1993 ACM-SIGMOD Conference on Management of Data*, Philadelphia, May.

Knuth, Donald. 1973. *The Art of Computer Programming,* Vol. 3, *Sorting and Searching,* Addison-Wesley, Reading, MA.

Korth, Henry, and Silberschatz, Abraham. 1986. *Database System Concepts*, 2nd ed., McGraw-Hill, New York.

Lucas, B., et al. 1992. "An Architecture for a Scientific Visualization System," *Proc. 1992 IEEE Visualization Conference*, Boston, October.

Melton, Jim (editor). 1995. ANSI SQL3 papers SC21 N9463 through SC21 N9467, ANSI SC21 Secretariat, +1.212.642.4900, New York.

Nievergelt, J., et al. 1984. "The Grid File: An Adaptable, Symmetric Multikey File Structure," *ACM Transactions on Database Systems*, March.

Ogle, Virginia E., and Stonebraker, Michael. 1995. "Chabot: Retrieval from a Relational Database of Images," *IEEE Computer*, September.

Organick, E. 1972. *The Multics System: An Examination of its Structure*, MIT Press, Cambridge, MA.

Rasure, J., and Young, M. 1992. "An Open Environment for Image Processing Software Development," *Proceedings of 1992 SPIE Symposium on Electronic Image Processing*, February.

Robinson, J. 1981. "The K-D-B Tree: A Search Structure for Large Multidimensional Indexes," *Proc. 1981 ACM-SIGMOD Conference on Management of Data*, Ann Arbor, MI, May.

Sarawagi, S., and Stonebraker, M. 1994. "Efficient Organization of Large Multidimensional Arrays," *Proc. 1994 IEEE Data Engineering Conference*, Houston, February.

Selinger, P., et al. 1979. "Access Path Selection in a Relational Data Base System," *Proc. 1979 ACM-SIGMOD Conference on Management of Data*, Boston, June.

Teorey, Toby. 1994. *Database Modeling and Design: The Entity-Relationship Approach,* Morgan Kaufmann, San Francisco.

Ullman, Jeffrey. 1980. *Principles of Database Systems*, Computer Science Press, Potomac, MD.

Upson, C. 1989. "The Application Visualization System," *IEEE Computer Graphics and Applications*, July.

Wahbe, Robert, Lucco, Steven, Anderson,Thomas, and Graham, Susan. 1993. "Efficient Software-Based Fault Isolation," *Proceedings of the 14th Symposium on Operating System Principles*, Asheville, NC, December.

Widom, Jennifer, and Ceri, Stefano.1995. *Active Database Systems*, Morgan Kaufmann, San Francisco.

Wong, E., and Katz, R. 1979. "Logical Design and Schema Conversion for Relational and DBTG Databases," *Proc. of the International Conference on the Entity-Relationship Approach*, Los Angeles, December.

Index

Related Titles from Morgan Kaufmann

Strategic Database Technology: Management for the Year 2000
Alan R. Simon

This comprehensive guide to emerging database technologies is a thorough investigation of the state of the art in database technology and the latest in research and development efforts. It's an essential source for IS managers, database administrators, systems analysts, and strategic planners.
ISBN 1-55860-264-X; paper; 446 pages; 1995.

The Object Database Standard: ODMG-93, Release 1.2
Edited by R. G. G. Cattell, with contributions from Tom Atwood, Douglas Barry, Jeff Eastman, Joshua Duhl, Guy Ferran, David Jordan, Mary Loomis, and Drew Wade

This book represents an important industry consensus on component technology for database products and languages that enables wide acceptance and adoption of object database technology. Highlights of this new release include significant SQL-92 compatibility enhancements to the coverage of Object Query Language, rigorous specifications and improvements to the coverage of C++ and Smalltalk binding, and a revised chapter defining the Object Model supported by ODMG-compliant implementations of object database management systems.
ISBN 1-55860-396-4; paper; 169 pages; 1995.

Additional Titles by Michael Stonebraker
Migrating Legacy Systems: Gateways, Interfaces & the Incremental Approach
Michael L. Brodie and Michael Stonebraker

An 11-step approach to incrementally migrate your legacy information system to a flexible IS that can support current and future business needs. A must for system administrators and technical managers to make their mission-critical application systems current and effective.
ISBN 1-55860-330-1; paper; 210 pages; 1995.

Readings in Database Systems, Second Edition
Edited by Michael Stonebraker

A comprehensive collection of 59 essential articles illustrating the depth and breadth of database technology. This selection of important research contributions is combined with Stonebraker's thoughtful and provocative introductions to offer insight on the most recent advances in database systems and their potential for future development.
ISBN 1-55860-252-6; paper; 970 pages; 1994.